HORRIBLE SCIENCE

SHOCKING ELECTRICITY

NICK ARNOLD

illustrated by
TONY DE SAULLES

■ SCHOLASTIC

Visit Nick Arnold at
www.nickarnold-website.com

And visit Tony De Saulles at
www.tonydesaulles.co.uk

Scholastic Children's Books,
Euston House, 24 Eversholt Street,
London, NW1 1DB, UK

A division of Scholastic Ltd
London ~ New York ~ Toronto ~ Sydney ~ Auckland
Mexico City ~ New Delhi ~ Hong Kong

First published in the UK by Scholastic Ltd, 2000
This edition published 2008

Text copyright © Nick Arnold, 2000
Illustrations © Tony De Saulles, 2000

ISBN 978 1407 10536 9

Printed and bound by CPI Group (UK) Ltd, Croydon, CR0 4YY

17 19 20 18

The right of Nick Arnold and Tony De Saulles to be identified as the author and
illustrator of this work respectively has been asserted by them in accordance with
the Copyright, Designs and Patents Act, 1988.

CONTENTS

A BATTERY HEN

SHOCKING JOKE

Nick Arnold has been writing stories and books since he was a youngster, but never dreamt he'd find fame writing about shocking electricity. His research involved swimming with an electric eel and collecting static electricity in his hair and he enjoyed every minute of it.

When he's not delving into Horrible Science, he spends his spare time eating pizza, riding his bike and thinking up corny jokes (though not all at the same time).

Tony De Saulles picked up his crayons when he was still in nappies and has been doodling ever since. He takes Horrible Science very seriously and even agreed to test how electricity runs through lightning. Fortunately, he has made a full recovery.

When he's not out with his sketchpad, Tony likes to write poetry and play squash, though he hasn't written any poetry about squash yet.

INTRODUCTION

Phew! It's the end of another day...

Mind you, science is boring – especially the science of electricity. That's SHOCKINGLY boring. So the alien monster probably got bored out of its two tentacle brains.

OddblOb the Blurb

► STAR-DATE: Present

MISSION: Observation of humanoid activity on planet known as "Earth".

GALAXY CO-ORDINATES:
0001.1100.0011100.0

BACKGROUND: Juvenile humanoids or "children" are subjected to factual information by adult humanoids at a gathering known as a "science lesson". Tests reveal that 99 per cent of data is forgotten by the children. This can result in a primitive display of aggression by the adult humanoid.

J.H.

A.H.

PRESENT ACTIVITY: Monitoring of "science lesson" in a primitive shelter known as a "school".

BRAINSCAN VIDEO

TODAY'S TOPIC IS ELECTRICITY

DRIBBLE! DOZE! YAWN!

NOTES: Juvenile humanoids enter an altered state of awareness known as "snoozing".

REPORT CONCLUSION: Total breakdown of communication is a frequent feature of the "science lesson".

Are your science lessons this bad? Does learning about electricity leave you in shock? Well, if science makes you suffer then reading this book could change your life. These pages are buzzing with shocking facts about electricity and humming with shocking stories including: the scientist who got struck by lightning, the surgeon who gave an electric shock to a gory human heart and the scientist who had a man *killed* to win an argument. After all, who needs *boring* science when you can have HORRIBLE Science?!

So what are you waiting for? Why not plug in and switch over to the next page!

SHOCKING ELECTRICAL POWER

This book is guaranteed free from electrical failure. Er – well, that's probably because it doesn't run on electricity unlike lots of other things – like toasters and televisions and fans and fridges. Where would we be without electricity? Well, you could be on a HORRIBLE SCIENCE HOLIDAY – just take a look at this:

A HOLIDAY WITH A DIFFERENCE!

THE REMOTE ISLAND OF

HORRA

THE ISLAND OF HORRA IS SO REMOTE THAT IT HAS NO ELECTRICITY

"There were none of these noisy CD thingummies - it was so peaceful I could hear my knitting needles click."

Mrs Edna Scruples (aged 97)

THE SMALL PRINT: HORRA IS A BIT CHILLY BUT AT LEAST IT DOESN'T RAIN MORE THAN ONCE A DAY (AND THEN ONLY FOR 24 HOURS).

So you don't fancy a bit of Horra? Well *tough* – it looks like you and your whole class are going there anyway – on a field trip.

Horra Towers
Horra

Dear Coastal Rescue
Please rescue us from Horrible Horra!

This island has <u>NO ELECTRICITY</u> and no electric heaters. It's <u>FREEZING</u> cold and we're taking turns to warm ourselves on the island's cat. All we've got to eat is cat food because our food supplies have been lost. And it's not even hot cat food because there aren't any electric cookers.

Our only light is a smelly candle – 'cos light bulbs need electricity. And it's <u>MEGA-BORING</u> here 'cos there's no TV, no videos, no computer games, and no CD player 'cos, yeah, you guessed it – they all need <u>ELECTRICITY</u>. And our teacher, Mr Sparks, is making us do extra homework. He says as a reward we can listen to him playing his squeaky old mouth organ. Laugh, we nearly cried.

You've got to come before we all die!!!! Pleeeeeeease!

Lots of love,
Class 5e

PS The cat would like some fresh fish for supper.

Yep, life without electricity sounds as much fun as cleaning a toilet with a toothbrush. But what do you actually know about this vital form of power? Heard any of these facts before?

FOUR SHOCKING FACTS ABOUT ELECTRICITY

1 You can make electricity from farts. It's true – by burning methane gas (found in some farts) you make heat which can be used to power generators and make electricity. Methane is also found in rotting rubbish, and in the United States there are 100 power stations based at rubbish tips that burn the gas.

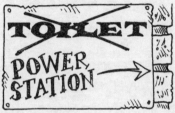

2 Lightning is a giant electrical spark (look out for the striking facts on page 58). One place that's safe from a lightning strike is inside a metal object like a car. The lightning runs through the metal but not through the air inside – so if you avoid touching the metal yourself you're safe. Much safer than sheltering in an outdoor toilet, for example.

3 Sometimes electrical power can surge when the power station pumps out too much electricity. (Imagine a huge wave of power surging into your sockets.) In 1990 people in the English village of Piddlehinton (yes, that's the name) were shocked when a power surge blew up their cookers and TVs.

4 The biggest power cut in history hit the north-east United States and Ontario, Canada in 1965. Thirty million people were plunged into darkness, but luckily only two were killed in the confusion.

Now you can test your knowledge further in this quickie quiz. It's bound to spark your interest.

SHOCKING QUIZ
1 Which of these machines *doesn't* need electricity to work?
a) The toilet
b) The telephone
c) The radio
2 Why is it that the victim of a huge electric shock gets thrown through the air? (No need to test this on family pets or frail elderly teachers.)
a) The force of the electricity lifts them off the ground.
b) The electric current runs through the nerves and

makes the muscles jerk violently so the victim leaps backwards.

c) Electricity reverses the force of gravity and makes the body weightless for a second.

3 Your teacher gets struck by lightning in the playground during a storm. Why is it dangerous to be in the playground at the same time?

a) You might have to give your teacher the kiss of life.

b) The playground will be wet from rain. The electric current from the lightning can spread through the wet surface and give you a nasty shock.

c) The hot lightning turns playground puddles into dangerous super-heated steam.

Answers:

1 a) Even if the radio doesn't work off mains electricity it will be powered by electricity from a battery. When you're chatting on the phone to a friend the receiver turns your voice into electric signals that travel down the wire to your friend's phone where they're changed into sounds again. Got all that? Toilets aren't powered by electricity but you may be interested to know that in 1966 inventor Thomas J Bayard devised an electrically powered wobbling toilet seat. The idea was that pummelling the bum prevents constipation. Sadly, people poo-poohed the idea and the seat went off the market.

2 b) This is handy because the person is usually thrown a safe distance from the object that's giving them the shock. Another effect of a violent shock to the muscles and nerves is to make you poo and pee ... resulting in shockingly smelly underwear.

3 b) Electricity can pass through water – which is why it is extremely silly to put any electrical machine (not designed for it) near water or to touch power sockets or switches with wet fingers.

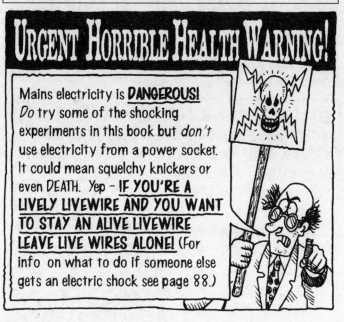

URGENT HORRIBLE HEALTH WARNING!

Mains electricity is **DANGEROUS!** *Do* try some of the shocking experiments in this book but *don't* use electricity from a power socket. It could mean squelchy knickers or even DEATH. Yep – **IF YOU'RE A LIVELY LIVEWIRE AND YOU WANT TO STAY AN ALIVE LIVEWIRE LEAVE LIVE WIRES ALONE!** (For info on what to do if someone else gets an electric shock see page 88.)

But before you get stuck into those experiments here's an important and interesting question: What on Earth is electricity actually *made of*? If you don't know read on – the answer's in the next shocking chapter!

13

SHOCKING ELECTRICAL SECRETS

OK, so what *is* electricity made of? Hands up who knows…

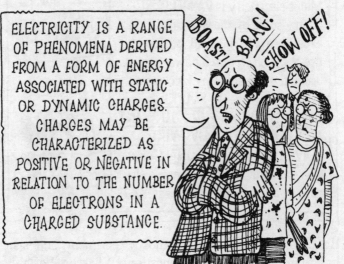

Oh dear, it looks like Mr Sparks, the science teacher, knows the answer:

ELECTRICITY IS A RANGE OF PHENOMENA DERIVED FROM A FORM OF ENERGY ASSOCIATED WITH STATIC OR DYNAMIC CHARGES. CHARGES MAY BE CHARACTERIZED AS POSITIVE OR NEGATIVE IN RELATION TO THE NUMBER OF ELECTRONS IN A CHARGED SUBSTANCE.

Well, thank you, Mr Sparks. Anyone understand that?

No? OK, let's try again. Everything in the universe is made of titchy bits called atoms and most atoms are surrounded by a cloud of even smaller blips of energy called electrons.

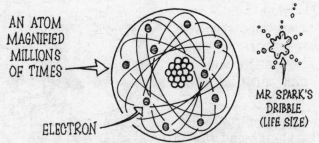

AN ATOM MAGNIFIED MILLIONS OF TIMES →

ELECTRON

MR SPARK'S DRIBBLE (LIFE SIZE)

The electricity in your power sockets is actually *made of* moving electrons and the *power* of electricity comes from the force the electrons give out.

Let's imagine an atom as a family...

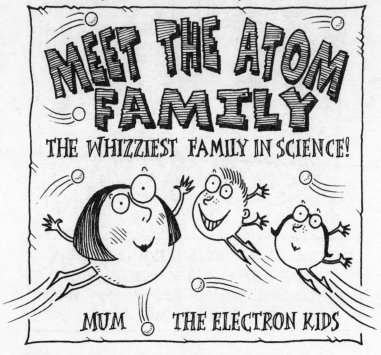

MEET THE ATOM FAMILY
THE WHIZZIEST FAMILY IN SCIENCE!

MUM   THE ELECTRON KIDS

16

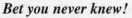

Bet you never knew!

Electrons really are tiny. An electron is ten thousand times smaller than the nucleus. If you had a very steady hand you could put 1,000,000,000,000 (one thousand billion) electrons in a line and even then you wouldn't have quite enough to stretch across a pinhead!

IT'S A WOBBLY LINE, SMITH. START AGAIN

IT'S A NUMBERS GAME

- Got a torch? All right then, switch it on and start counting – 1, 2, 3...
- That dim feeble light in your torch bulb uses 6,280,000,000,000,000,000 – (6.28 billion billion) electrons *every second*. Just to give you some idea of how massive this number is...
- A school day has about 23,400 seconds – if you don't believe me try counting them! So if you wanted to get to a million you'd have to count non-stop for another ten days.

...EIGHT HUNDRED AND SEVENTY TWO THOUSAND, THREE HUNDRED AND NINETY ONE...

- If you kept counting for another 32 years and 354 days (and that means counting whilst eating and

17

sleeping and going to the toilet) you'd eventually reach one billion (if you hadn't died of boredom).

- Not gobsmacked yet? Well, get this… In order to count those electrons used by your dim and feeble little torch *in just one second* you should have started counting well before the Earth was formed 4,600 million years ago!

A NOTE TO THE READER…

What we call an "electric current" is actually a stream of electrons flowing through a wire – this is measured in amps. Can you imagine what it would be like to *swim* in this stream? Here's a story about a person who did just that. He's an odd-job worker called Andy Mann – good name, eh? It all began when Andy got a shrinking feeling and was made to feel very very small...

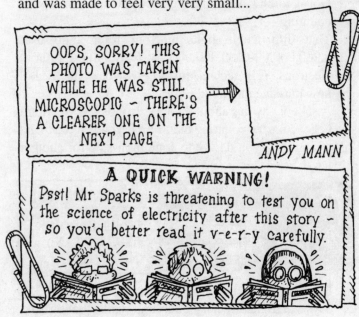

IT'S A SMALL, SMALL, SMALL, SMALL WORLD

Here's me story and I want cash up front, OK? Me name is Andy Mann - Andy by name, handy by nature, geddit?

ANDY MANN
General Repairs,
Plumbing, Electrics,
Brickwork

Need a handy man? -
Andy's your man!
No job too small!

(Ring 01201 5843673 mobile 09123 87690)

You can call me anytime but not when there's darts on the telly. Yeah, I was telling you what happened - it all started when I went round to Professor Buzzoff's house to do a job. Just a bit of sanitary engineering as we say in the trade - well, she had a blocked toilet pipe.

Anyway, imagine me surprise when she said I had to wear this protective suit.

"All right," I said - thinking the toilet might be a "stinker", as we say in the trade.

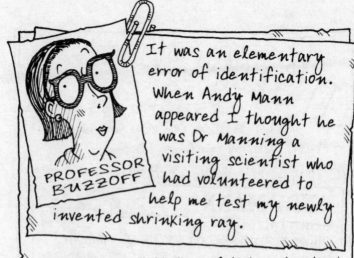

It was an elementary error of identification. When Andy Mann appeared I thought he was Dr Manning a visiting scientist who had volunteered to help me test my newly invented shrinking ray.

PROFESSOR BUZZOFF

Dr Manning - huh! The Prof told me to stand under this machine. It didn't look much like a toilet and I was about to say that the wiring looked a bit dodgy and did she want it seeing to when she flicked a lever. Then she started getting bigger and the room started getting bigger. But hold on ... *it was me getting smaller!*

ER! EH? OOER! YIKES! ERK!

Well I know me card says no job's too small, but this job was looking, well ... a bit too small. So I went on shrinking until I got sucked into an electrical wire. "Wire am I here?" I asked meself.

There was a malfunction in the diminisher unit. By the time I managed to de-activate the ray Andy had shrunk to 0.000000025 mm, almost as small as an atom. And to make matters worse he had vanished inside the machine. Obviously this was a situation of some danger.

Yeah well, it was dangerous all right. The first thing I saw was these weird balls and I thought blimey they're atoms. And there was these tiny blips buzzing round the atoms. They were so fast they looked like a blurry mist. Well, the Prof later said they were electrons. The wire looked like this huge tunnel with atoms round the sides and there was electrons flowing through it like a river. Then I got swept away by them electrons. They was like rubbery peas and I had to swim for my life. Was I scared? Yeah, I was wetting meself. How d'you get out of this electric current Andy?

Well, me being a skilled electrician (all jobs considered by the way), I knew that an electric current is made by electrons all flowing one way. And those electrons was fast. Luckily they missed me or I would have been KILLED until I was DEAD!

Fascinating! The electrons were zapping at 1 million metres per second, and electrical signals can zip along at nearly the speed of light! Meanwhile I frantically tried to reset the shrinking ray to make Andy bigger. I switched on the light to help me see.

CLICK!

Yeah well, guess what happened? The wire got narrower. All the electrons squashed together and they slowed down and started rubbing against the atoms around the sides - yeah, and me. Phew - it was hot! Well, it's friction innit? Rubbing makes heat like when you rub your hands together.

SWEAT

ELECTRONS

ATOMS

Blobs of light started flying around - and then it hit me. *I WAS INSIDE THE LIGHT BULB.* Yeah - the one she'd just switched on. Mind you, I wasn't feeling too bright.

Of course, I didn't know that Andy was in the bulb. We scientists call the friction Andy describes "resistance" and the blobs of light Andy saw are called "photons" (fo-tonns).

PHOTON MAGNIFIED MILLIONS OF TIMES

They're given off by the electrons as they try to cool down. It must have been a scientifically fascinating experience.

Yeah fascinating, Prof - shame I was about to DIE! Me protective suit was melting and I reckoned I'd be melting soon! I was boiling hot and sweating buckets. "This is it, Andy," I said to meself, "I'll never get to see the darts final!"

Just then me mobile rang. I didn't feel too chatty ... but I answered it anyway ... might as well say goodbye to someone.

RING!

I observed Andy's business card and remembered he had a mobile phone. So I called his number. I was shocked to discover that he was inside the light bulb and switched it off immediately. The switch stopped the flow of electrons and the light went out.

Just in time! The wire started to cool down - but I wasn't out of the woods yet - I mean out of the wire. I mean how was the Prof s'posed to get me out? Maybe I was going to stay tiny all me life. How was I s'posed to live? I couldn't even go outside cos an ant might tread on me and squash me flat! ARGH!

It took me three hours to enlarge the bulb wire in small steps and each time I cut out the portion of wire that contained Andy until eventually he was free. Then I was able to enlarge him back to his correct size. Of course, he was rather annoyed...

I'M IN THIS BIT!

A quick note

Good news! We've managed to lock Mr Sparks in the stationery cupboard so there won't be a science test – Phew!

But just in case he manages to escape here's a quick crib sheet with all the science test answers on.

Electricity Test
Answers

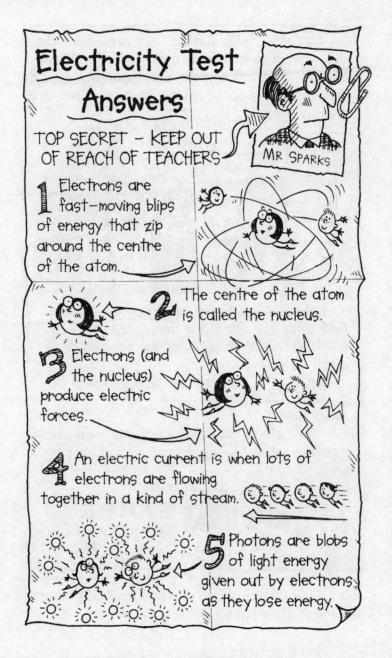

MR SPARKS

1 Electrons are fast-moving blips of energy that zip around the centre of the atom.

2 The centre of the atom is called the nucleus.

3 Electrons (and the nucleus) produce electric forces.

4 An electric current is when lots of electrons are flowing together in a kind of stream.

5 Photons are blobs of light energy given out by electrons as they lose energy.

6 Resistance is when electrons start to rub against atoms and slow down in a wire. Resistance is also used to make heat in special wires that heat water in electric kettles and give out heat from hairdryers and electric heaters.

HAS THE KETTLE BOILED?

IT'S PUTTING UP RESISTANCE.

SHOCKING EXPRESSIONS

DO YOU KNOW ANY GOOD CONDUCTORS?

Do you say...?

WELL THERE'S MY MUSIC TEACHER. BUT SHE'S A TERRIBLE CONDUCTOR - THAT'S WHY THE SCHOOL ORCHESTRA IS SO BAD.

By now you might be bursting to ask a question. Well, I don't know that for sure – you might be bursting for a pee. Anyway, your question might go like this...

IF ELECTRONS ARE SO SMALL, HOW WERE THEY EVER DISCOVERED?

GOOD QUESTION

Well, why not discover the next electrifying chapter and find out...?

SHOCKING DISCOVERIES

One of the most amazing things about science is the way scientists calmly tell us that tiny things exist even though no one has ever seen them.

Well, lets face it they're both far too tiny to see even with the most powerful microscopes. But here's the amazing story of how it was discovered (that's the electron not your teacher's brain)...

TWO REALLY BIG BREAKTHROUGHS

By 1880 scientists knew how to make it and they knew how to store it (see page 55) but they didn't know what electricity was actually made of. In that year scientist William Crookes built a new machine to help him find the answer...

CATHODE RAY TUBE

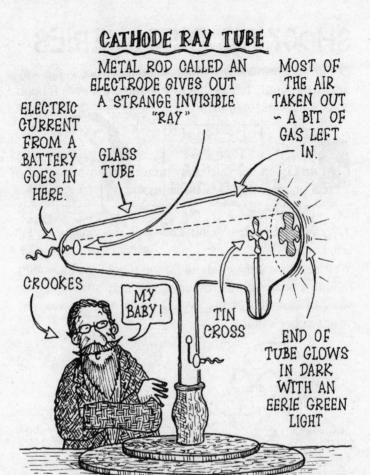

QUICK SCIENTIFIC NOTE...

By taking the air out of the container Crookes was getting rid of atoms in the air that might get in the way of the invisible ray. We now know that the "ray" was in fact a stream of electrons shooting out from the battery.

COULD YOU BE A SCIENTIST?

So what do you think made the green glow?

a) The gas glowing as it's hit by the electrons.

b) The glass tube glowing where the electrons hit it.

c) A chemical reaction between the gas and the chemicals in the glass.

Answer: b) The electrons hit the atoms of the glass and heated them up until they gave out energy in the form of light photons.

Of course, Crookes didn't know all this and he didn't understand what he was seeing. And as you're about to discover it was hard for Crookes to explain his work to other scientists because they didn't trust him. The problem was that, unlike most scientists, Crookes believed in *ghosts*. Here's his story...

Hall of fame: William Crookes (1832–1919) Nationality: British

Crookes was the oldest of 16 kids. (Would you like 15 cheeky little brothers and sisters breaking your things?)

Obviously this could drive a person to desperate measures and maybe that's why Crookes became a chemistry teacher. But eventually he inherited a fortune. (So at least he could afford Christmas presents for everyone.)

31

He retired from teaching and set up his own private chemistry lab for exciting experiments.

But some of his investigations shocked other scientists. In those days many people believed that the spirits of the dead came back as ghosts and could be summoned by people with special abilities called mediums. Crookes decided to find the truth by careful scientific observation…

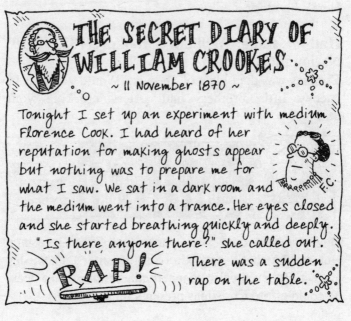

THE SECRET DIARY OF WILLIAM CROOKES

~ 11 November 1870 ~

Tonight I set up an experiment with medium Florence Cook. I had heard of her reputation for making ghosts appear but nothing was to prepare me for what I saw. We sat in a dark room and the medium went into a trance. Her eyes closed and she started breathing quickly and deeply.

"Is there anyone there?" she called out.

There was a sudden rap on the table.

RAP!

"Rap once for yes," demanded the medium.
Bang!
"Are you a spirit?"
Another rap.
"Can you make yourself visible?"
I asked, sounding rather scared.
A cold wind blew through the room. The curtain fluttered and I saw a vague white shape. I blinked in horror – it was a woman with a ghostly pale face. She drifted round the room and I almost managed to touch her unearthly form.
"Who ... what are you?" I gasped.
The ghost moved her pale lips. In a faint voice she replied: "My name is Katie, I have a message for you..."
The medium gave a sudden cry. She was pale and sweaty now, and when I looked again the ghost had vanished. So what was the message? I can't wait for the next session!

But had he seen a real ghost? Crookes' fellow scientists were less than impressed with his work as a spectre inspector. Most scientists don't believe in ghosts (I suppose they can see right through them) and they thought that Crookes didn't stand a ghost of a chance of proving anything. Instead the investigation ruined Crookes' image as a sensible scientist.

One scientist who didn't give up on Crookes was John Joseph Thomson (1856–1940), a professor at Cambridge University. JJ, as his friends called him, was useless at experiments and usually broke his equipment (but blowing up the school lab is not always a sign of genius as I'm sure your teacher will point out). Luckily for JJ, when he became a professor he had people to do the hands-on work for him.

JJ thought the "ray" Crookes had reported might be made of tiny blips of energy and to find out more he repeated one of Crookes' tests of using a magnet to bend the ray. He worked out how strong the magnetic force had to be to bend the ray and using complicated maths he calculated the weight of the blips that he thought made up the ray from the angle it was bent. Try doing that for your maths homework!

It turned out the ray really *was* made of tiny blips and they were far lighter than the lightest atoms. Thomson calculated how much energy each blip carried and realized that it matched the lightest atoms. Thomson reckoned rightly that each atom carried at least one and usually far more of the blips. The tiny blips, of course, were electrons.

Bet you never knew!
Electrons make things feel solid. You see, the electrical force made by an electron pushes other electrons away. Solid objects are made of atoms and electrons tightly packed together and so when you squash them they push apart slightly and this makes the object feel solid. Just think – if it wasn't for electrons, sitting on a chair would be like sitting on a slimy school dinner blancmange. You'd sink through it and end up sprawled on your bum.

ELECTRONS – WHO NEEDS 'EM?

SPLOSH!

Electric forces can do lots of other interesting things. They can even make your hair stand on end! And you can find out how in the next chapter – it's bound to set a few sparks flying.

I'D BETTER READ ON...

SHOCKING STATIC ELECTRICITY

Have you ever got an electric shock when stroking the cat or trying on a woolly jumper? Yes? CONGRATULATIONS – you've encountered static electricity. But "static" is definitely the wrong word. After all "static" means staying still...

So you'd think that in static electricity the electrons must be lazing around reading comics. WRONG! Actually, although the electrons aren't all flowing together in an electric current, they're still whizzing around as usual. And in static electricity the electrons also get to fly through the air and make sparks and give scientists nasty shocks and many other exciting things.

Wanna know more?

Before you can understand the secret of static you need to get your brain-box round the electrical forces made by an electron and the atom nucleus. This quickie experiment should help...

Dare you discover ... how electric forces work?

You will need:
Two magnets

What you do:
Put them close together.

What happens...?
a) The magnets spring apart or pull together depending on which way round they are.
b) The magnets are *always* drawn together.
c) The magnets can be placed together but you don't feel any force between them.

Answer: a) When the magnets spring apart you can imagine that they are two electrons. As you may recall from page 35 the electrons are pushed apart by their own forces.

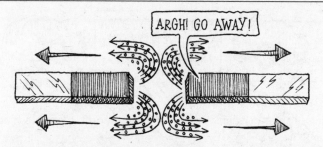

When the magnets pull together you can imagine they're like an electron and a nucleus. This time their

37

forces actually pull them together! (It's all to do with complex interactions between the two forces and no, I don't understand this either.)

SHOCKING EXPRESSIONS

Two scientists are talking...

Are they comparing hotel bills?

Now here's another glimpse of our pals the Atom family as they show you how they make static electricity...

THE ATOM FAMILY IN...
STATIC SUSPENSE

The adventure begins with a scientist who is about to make static electricity.

WE'LL NEED A BALLOON AND A CAT.

1 We rub the balloon on the cat's fur ten times or more.

THAT'S QUITE NICE, ACTUALLY.

2 The Atom family are living on the cat's fluff.

The atoms of the balloon are rubbing electrons free from the atoms of the cat fluff. Here's a close-up view of what happens to them...

3 The electrons are now stranded on the balloon's surface. Of course this means there's a lot of electron energy (negative charge, remember?) on the balloon.

4 The powerful negative charge made by the electrons results in a negative force that tries to pull on the atoms of the cat's fluff.

5 Meanwhile on the cat's fluff, the atoms that are missing their electrons are positively charged. And together their positive electrical forces try to pull the electrons back.

6 These forces make the cat's fur stand up on end as they try to pull the balloon and cat together.

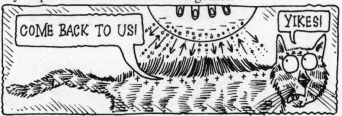

7 When the balloon is brought nearer to the cat's fur the missing electrons are yanked back to their atoms. You can even hear this happen as a quiet crackle.

Bet you never knew!
Ancient Greek boffin Thales of Miletus (624–545 BC) made static electricity by rubbing amber (a kind of fossil tree gum) with an old bit of fur (I hate to think what happened to his pet cat). The amber could then pick up feathers.

Well, if that's sparked your interest maybe you'd like to try that experiment too (hopefully your cat will manage to keep her fur on).

Or maybe you'd like to try this experiment...

Dare you discover ... how to make clingfilm move?

You will need:

Two pieces of new clingfilm 10 cm x 2 cm
A clean dry comb
Blutak
Some clean hair – you might possibly find some on your head. (If not maybe you could ask the cat nicely.)

What you do:

1 Hold a piece of clingfilm in each hand. Try to bring the two pieces of clingfilm together. Notice what happens.

2 Stick a piece of clingfilm to the end of a table so the clingfilm hangs downwards. Now comb your hair quickly and strongly four times. Quickly point the teeth of the comb towards the strip of clingfilm and hold it close but not touching. Notice what happens.

Well, what does happen?

a) The two pieces of clingfilm are drawn together. But the clingfilm doesn't want to touch the comb.

b) The pieces of clingfilm don't want to touch but the clingfilm does want to touch the comb.

c) A spark flies between the clingfilm and comb but nothing happens between the two bits of clingfilm.

Answer: b) The atoms of the clingfilm are short of electrons. This means they are positively charged and give out positive forces. Remember how two negative forces push each other away? Well, two positive forces also push against each other and that's why the pieces of clingfilm move apart. The comb rips electrons off your hairs and the force from these electrons (negative charge) pulls in the positively charged atoms in the clingfilm.

SUPER STATIC

Static electricity is shockingly useful. For example, did you know that photocopiers use static electricity to copy documents?

Here's what happens...

1 A bright light shines on the picture to be copied and its image reflects on to a mirror and through a lens on to a metal drum. Got all that?

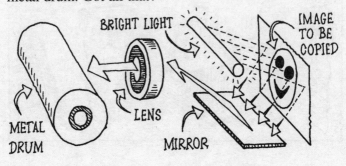

BRIGHT LIGHT

IMAGE TO BE COPIED

METAL DRUM

LENS

MIRROR

2 The drum is coated with a substance called selenium (see-leen-nee-um) that gives off electrons when light shines on it.

3 This means the areas of the drum that get most light (in other words the brighter parts of the original) lose negatively charged electrons and become positively charged. Yep – it pays to think positive!

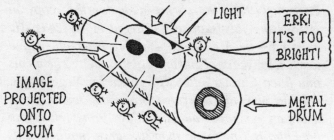

4 Positively charged toner powder gets sprinkled on the drum and sticks to the dark areas which are still negatively charged. (Hope you're taking notes on all this.)

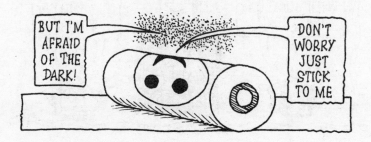

5 Paper now goes over the drum and the toner sticks to the paper to make a copy of the original picture.

6 A heater softens the toner and squashes it on to the paper.

7 *Finito* – one perfect photocopy!

Bet you never knew!

The photocopier was invented by US inventor Chester Carlson (1906–1968) who made his first copy in 1938 using tiny statically charged moss seeds. He must have been ex-static – ha ha. After all, it had taken four years of tinkering with smelly chemicals that filled Chester's flat with rotten farty egg whiffs. On the way his marriage broke up, his research assistant resigned, and countless firms refused to back him. But after more than 20 years of improvements photocopiers became popular and Chester became a multi-millionaire.

But Chester's discovery wouldn't have been possible without the work of earlier scientists who investigated static electricity. Did you know some of the most shocking static electricity experiments were performed by a scientist called Stephen Gray (1666–1736)? And can you believe he conducted these experiments on ... helpless children. Now read on for the whole shocking story...

A SHOCKING STORY

London 1730

"You new here?" asked Joe.

The thin little girl with the dirty face nodded dumbly.

"And that's why you were following me about just now?"

The girl nodded again.

Joe chewed his lip as he pondered what to do. He didn't want some little kid following him around all day but he could see the new girl was scared of being in the children's home.

They sat down cross-legged on the bare dusty floor and he asked her name.

"Hannah." the girl whispered as if scared to raise her voice.

"Well Hannah, it's not so bad in here. Look, I tell you what, here's a story to take your mind off it."

The girl leaned forward expectantly.

"Is it a true story?"

"It's true all right," said Joe. "I was working for this scientist and guess what – he did experiments on me!"

"You mean it – actual science experiments?" asked the girl.

"Stop asking questions and I'll tell you. It happened one day when this old scientist geezer came to the children's home and asked for a kid to help him with his work. He was fat and rich and his name was Mr Gray, Mr Stephen Gray.

"Well, the supervisor collared me and took me to Mr Gray's place. Real posh it was with heavy curtains and a smell of polish and silver on the table. And guess what? Mr Gray gave me a slap-up meal! Said I looked as if I could do with feeding! I had beef and onions and dumplings and potatoes and gravy and three helpings of pudding. Heaven it was."

Joe glanced at Hannah and sure enough she was drooling. "I want to work for Mr Gray too!" she said hungrily.

"Mr Gray's servant came in. She was this really old grim-looking woman named Mrs Salter, and she said 'If the boy eats any more he will break his cords.' *Cords*? I thought. Well, that made me a bit scared. Maybe this Gray bloke was going to tie me up and then he was going to *kill* me. *Maybe he was going to chop my body up and eat me!*

"Mr Gray must have seen my expression because he patted me on the head and said 'Don't worry Joseph, it won't hurt much.'"

"Did it hurt?" asked Hannah fearfully.

"Well," said Joe bravely, "I'm still alive, ain't I? Anyway, Mr Gray took me into this room and I was gobsmacked. It was stacked with all these scientific gadgets, like glass rods, a set of metal balls – I didn't know what they was for – and flasks and telescopes.

"Mr Gray picked up a telescope. 'I used to be an astronomer till I did my back in bending over that telescope. Well, now I'm into electricity.'

"'What's electricity?' I asked, and Mr Gray told me all about this weird force. Well, don't ask me to explain it. I couldn't get me head round it.

"'Is that anything to do with them metal balls?' I mumbled stupidly.

"'Ah yes – interesting they are,' said Mr Gray. 'I proved that it doesn't matter if a ball is hollow or solid – it can still store the same amount of static electricity. I think the force must be stored on the outside of the ball. And I learnt how to electrify objects and that brings us to our experiment.'

"He nodded to Mrs Salter and quick as a flash she looped silk cords round my shoulders and legs and waist. I was too surprised to say anything. But I yelled loud enough when they hoisted me into the air. I thought me dinner was going to come up all over the floor.

"Mr Gray put his finger on his lips. 'Don't shout, Joseph. We're only going to electrify you.'

"'But I don't want to be electrified!' I yelled.

"Mr Gray looked troubled. 'But it's for science, Joseph and anyway, I'll pay you sixpence.'

"Well, that settled it. I'd have done it for a penny.

"I felt really weird like I was swimming – or maybe flying in the air with my arms outstretched on either side. Mrs Salter rubbed my clothes real hard with a glass rod

– blimey was she strong! Meanwhile Mr Gray put some tiny bits of paper on three metal plates on the ground under me.

"'Now, Joseph,' said Mr Gray, 'reach out your hands and pick up those bits of paper.'

"'I can't do that!' I cried. My arms were too short to reach the paper and just to show him I tried. And something magic happened. The bits of paper flew towards my fingers – they looked just like confetti at a wedding.

"'Bravo!' shouted Mr Gray clapping his big fat hands and I was so chuffed I gave him a mid-air bow.

"'Can I come down now?' I asked. Mr Gray nodded and his servant reached out to untie me. There was a sudden crack and I felt a sharp pain. It was agony!

"'Oh dear,' said Mr Gray, 'you seem to have received an electric shock. Never mind here's your sixpence.'"

"You really got a whole sixpence?" asked Hannah, her eyes widening.

"Yes," said Joseph proudly.

"That's a lot of money. I've never seen one. Can I see it? Can I touch it?"

Joe held the shining silver coin and the girl touched his hand.

"Ow!" she yelled. "You stung me!"

"Don't worry," said the boy with a careless wave of his hand. "It's just an electric shock."

Dare you discover ... how Joe picked up the paper?

You will need:

A piece of polystyrene (to represent Joe)
A woollen jumper or pair of nylon tights
A few tiny bits of paper (the circles of paper from a hole punch are ideal)

What you do:

1 Rub the polystyrene on the fabric a few times.
2 Hold the polystyrene near the bits of paper.

What happens?

a) The bits of paper jump on to the polystyrene.
b) You get an electric shock.
c) The polystyrene is pulled gently towards the paper.

Answer: a) When Joe was rubbed with the rod, the glass removed electrons from his clothes and skin. This gave the atoms that made them up a positive charge. The electrons in the paper were pulled towards him and this pulled the paper too. When Mrs Salter touched Joe electrons from her skin also rushed on to Joe and gave him a shock.

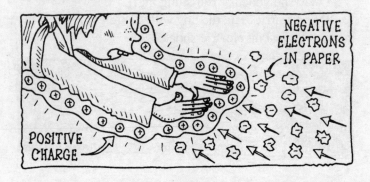

52

Oh, by the way, Hannah didn't get a shock because Joe was still electrified – it's just that skin sometimes collects an electric charge (for example when you walk over a carpet). That's why you can get a shock by touching people.

IT'S SUCH A SHOCK TO MEET YOU!

Bet you never knew!
Besides electrifying a boy, Gray found he could electrify hair and feathers. It's even said that he sent electricity along gold-painted cow guts. (Don't ask me what he was doing painting cow guts gold!)

SIXPENCE? I'LL WANT A LOT MORE THAN THAT, PAL!

He investigated different conductors (and if you don't know what they are check back to page 28 at once!).

SO WHAT HAPPENED NEXT?
In 1732 brave French scientist Charles Dufay (1698–1739) repeated Gray's experiment using himself instead

of a boy. According to one story, when Dufay's assistant tried to touch him, the scientist got a shock that burnt through his waistcoat.

The scientist found the experience thrilling – or should I say electrifying (ha ha) – and insisted on repeating it in the dark so that he could see the spark made by the static electricity.

Dufay's experiments proved that anything could be electrically charged by rubbing except for liquids, metals and a grisly lump of meat. Dufay didn't realize this, but since these substances are good conductors of electricity, electrons tend to run through them rather than sticking around to build up a powerful negative electric charge.

Within a few years scientists developed brilliant machines that could make and store static electricity if it was needed for experiments. (In those days mains electricity hadn't been invented.) Would you fancy owning one of these machines? Of course you wouldn't use it to give nasty shocks to your teacher/brother/sister would you? WOULD YOU?

A SHOCKING CATALOGUE

Amaze your friends and shock your enemies with this incredible range of static electricity generators from SPARKY-JOLT LTD.

You'll love a Leyden Jar!

Developed by Dutch scientist Pieter van Musschenbroek (1692–1761) this stylish jar stores static electricity.

METAL BALL

METAL CHAIN

WATER IN GLASS JAR

STATIC ELECTRICITY PASSES DOWN METAL CHAIN INTO JAR AND CAN'T ESCAPE.

SHOCKING SAFETY WARNING!

Touch the metal ball at the top and you'll get a painful electric shock. This shocking discovery was made accidentally by Musschenbroek's assistant. Ouch!

D'YOU MEAN THIS BIT?... ARGH!

X-RAY VIEW OF GLASS JAR WITH METAL LINING BOTH INSIDE AND OUT

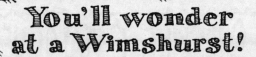

You'll wonder at a Wimshurst!

Named after its inventor James Wimshurst (1832-1903), this wonderful piece of electric wizardry makes static electricity when the glass and metal discs rub together.

GASP AS SPARKS LEAP BETWEEN THE BRASS BALLS!

METAL STRIPS COLLECT ELECTRIC CHARGE PRODUCED BY TURNING WHEEL

SCIENCE CRANK J.WIMSHURST

CRANK

GUARANTEED! . . . IF IT DOESN'T WORK THERE'S NO CHARGE!

COLLECTED CHARGE TRAVELS DOWN INTO LEYDEN JAR FOR STORAGE

TURN CRANK TO PRODUCE ELECTRIC CHARGE

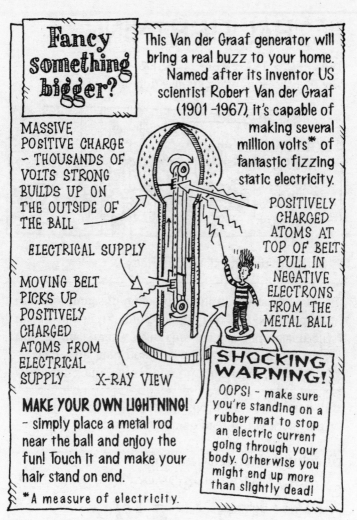

Fancy something bigger?

This Van der Graaf generator will bring a real buzz to your home. Named after its inventor US scientist Robert Van der Graaf (1901–1967), it's capable of making several million volts* of fantastic fizzing static electricity.

MASSIVE POSITIVE CHARGE – THOUSANDS OF VOLTS STRONG BUILDS UP ON THE OUTSIDE OF THE BALL

ELECTRICAL SUPPLY

MOVING BELT PICKS UP POSITIVELY CHARGED ATOMS FROM ELECTRICAL SUPPLY

POSITIVELY CHARGED ATOMS AT TOP OF BELT PULL IN NEGATIVE ELECTRONS FROM THE METAL BALL

X-RAY VIEW

MAKE YOUR OWN LIGHTNING! – simply place a metal rod near the ball and enjoy the fun! Touch it and make your hair stand on end.

SHOCKING WARNING!

OOPS! – make sure you're standing on a rubber mat to stop an electric current going through your body. Otherwise you might end up more than slightly dead!

*A measure of electricity.

Did anyone mention lightning? Well, you may be thunderstruck to discover that lightning is a form of static electricity. And if that came like a bolt from the blue you really ought to read the next chapter. You're bound to find it striking!

LETHAL LIGHTNING

TEACHER'S TEA-BREAK TEASER

Try this shockingly tricky question on your teacher...

HOW CAN WATER START A FIRE?

STAFF

Clue: it's to do with static electricity.

Answer: Sometimes when oil tanker holds are being cleaned with high pressure hoses, atoms in the water rub together really fast. This makes static electricity that results in lightning sparks. The sparks can set fire to petrol fumes in the hold and blow up the tanker!

But how do water drops make lightning? If you're a bright spark you'll read on and find out!

Shocking electricity fact file

NAME: Lightning

THE BASIC FACTS:
1 Inside a storm cloud violent winds rub together water drops and tiny lumps of ice.

RUB!

WATER

ICE

58

SWOOP!

NEGATIVELY CHARGED WATER

2 The ice loses electrons to the water and gets swept upwards.

3 The drops of water tend to fall downwards (yes – they're called rain) so the top of the cloud without electrons becomes positively charged and the bottom, with all those electrons, is negatively charged.

POSITIVE

NEGATIVE

YIKES!

RUMBLE!

+ + + + + + +

4 The powerful negative charge in the base of the cloud makes a force that pushes away negatively charged electrons on the ground. This leaves an area of positively charged atoms.

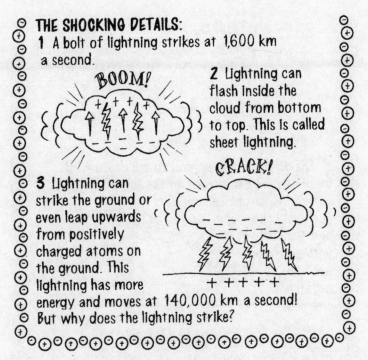

THE SHOCKING DETAILS:

1 A bolt of lightning strikes at 1,600 km a second.

BOOM!

2 Lightning can flash inside the cloud from bottom to top. This is called sheet lightning.

CRACK!

3 Lightning can strike the ground or even leap upwards from positively charged atoms on the ground. This lightning has more energy and moves at 140,000 km a second! But why does the lightning strike?

Obviously anyone who tries to find out is taking a very big risk – a VERY BIG RISK.

A FLASHY JOB

Professor Buzzoff wanted to film lightning in ultra-slow motion. But who could she ask to take on this ultra-dangerous job? There was only one person in the frame.

LEAVE IT OUT, PROF – I'M NOT DOING NO MORE SHRINKING!

I assured Andy that no shrinking was required and that I would join him on the shoot. After a brief discussion about money he agreed to take the job.

I took the job cos I'm a dab hand with camcorders. I do weddings, funerals, whatever (all offers considered). So filming lightning seemed a cinch - I mean, it's all over in a flash, innit? So there I was filming the clouds and waiting for a flash of lightning and I cricked me neck looking up and got a right soaking. "Water rotten job!" I said to meself...

Andy didn't have too long to wait. When the negative charge at the bottom of the cloud reaches a certain power, the lightning appears as a bright blob under the cloud. This is actually a ball of negatively charged electrons.

A stream of electrons flashes downwards, drawn by the pulling force of the positively charged atoms on the ground. What we call the streak of lightning marks the path taken by the electrons through the atoms of the air. On the way, the lightning hits atoms in the air making them give off heat and light. The lightning appears much brighter.

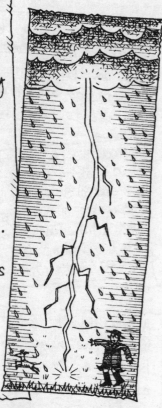

The lightning hits the ground. The bolt of lightning is up to 1 cm wide.

The lightning heats up the air around it very quickly, then it cools again very quickly. This creates shock waves in the air that our ears hear as thunder. As Andy was taking this picture I became aware that another bolt of lightning was forming in the cloud under which he was standing. . .

Did someone say "All over in a flash"? Didn't realize it would be over for _me_ in a flash. I was too busy filming the Prof (who was jumping up and down pointing to something high above me) to see the next streak coming. Fast as lightning it was. . . Argh!

THIS IS A NEWS FLASH. ANDY MANN HAS BEEN STRUCK BY LIGHTNING! WE'LL BE HEADING OVER TO THE HOSPITAL IN A FEW MINUTES TO CHECK ON HIS CONDITION.

So YOU'RE not scared of lightning? And you fancy making some lightning in the comfort of your own home? OK – here's how; but try not to fire your lightning at little brothers or sisters or the cat – Tiddles has suffered enough!

Dare you discover ... how to make lightning?

You will need:
A radio with the aerial extended
A balloon
A thick jumper (no not a stupid kangaroo – I mean a *woollen* jumper). A woollen rug or scarf will also do.

What you do:
1 Wait until it gets dark or sit in the coal cellar with the lights out. This experiment works best in complete darkness.

2 Rub the balloon on the wool about ten times. Put it near or touching the aerial.

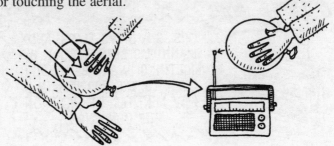

What do you see?
a) The radio comes on without you touching it – it's spooky.

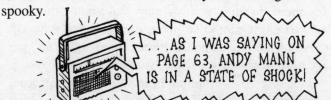

...AS I WAS SAYING ON PAGE 63, ANDY MANN IS IN A STATE OF SHOCK!

b) An eerie glowing ball of light appears and floats round the room – scaring the life out of your pet budgie.
c) Tiny sparks.

Dare you discover ... how to hear lightning?
You will need:
The same equipment from the first experiment

What you do:
1 Switch the radio to AM and make sure it's not tuned to any station.
2 Turn the volume down very low.
3 Repeat the first experiment and listen.

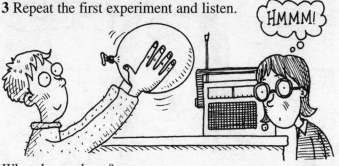

HMMM!

What do you hear?
a) Pop music even though the radio isn't tuned.
b) A quiet pop (but it isn't music).
c) You hear the sound in **b)** but it's REALLY LOUD.

Hall of fame: Benjamin Franklin (1706–1790)
Nationality: American

Benjamin Franklin packed so much into his life it's a wonder that he had time to eat or sleep. He was a...

Young Ben was the youngest of 17 children – can you imagine how terrible that must have been? Sixteen older brothers and sisters bossing you around and getting their baths first so you have to make do with their filthy scummy bath water? Ben had just three years of schooling but that must have seemed too long because he hated maths and failed all his tests. But worse was to follow – he had to spend the next seven years working 12 hours a day for no pay for one of his older brothers. Would you swap school for this?

Ben learnt the art of printing in his brother's shop. Then suddenly at the ripe old age of 15, he found himself a *newspaper editor.*

Ben's brother had been locked up for saying rude things about important people in the newspaper he printed. So Ben took charge of the newspaper and that must have been really cool. He could have printed wicked articles about computer games and rollerblading. If they'd been invented then, that is.

Ben eventually fell out with his brother and went to Philadelphia, arriving with just a small loaf of bread to eat and no money at all. Luckily, he soon found work as a printer and became pals with the British Governor who ruled the city in those days. But the Governor played a shocking trick on young Ben. He sent him to London to learn more about printing but after Ben set sail he realized that the Governor hadn't given him the money he'd promised.

Ben's big break came in 1732. He was back in Pennsylvania after a spell as a printer in London and he published an almanac – a sort of calendar with wise sayings. It was an instant smash-hit! The sayings are so well-known and wise you might have heard your granny use them...

Actually, Ben Franklin *didn't* take his own advice. When he lived in Paris in the 1770s he enjoyed lots of late-night parties, but he still remained healthy and rich, and as you're about to find out he was wise too. Mention this to your granny ... *if you dare*!

Ben made so much money he retired from printing and got interested in science and inventing things. Amongst other things he invented a new kind of wood-burning stove, extendable grippers for taking things off high shelves (and raiding the biscuit jar) and a musical instrument made of a glass bowl with a wet rim. The glass bowl turned round and if you touched the rim with your fingertips it made a sound.

Bet you never knew!
Benjamin Franklin was interested in everything – including farting. He set up a competition to discover a drug that could be mixed with food to make pleasant perfumed farts. Although such a discovery is not to be sniffed at, sadly there were no winners.

But Ben's greatest discoveries were to do with electricity. In 1746 he went to a science talk on electricity and he was so thrilled by it that he bought up all the lecturer's equipment and started doing his own experiments.

Like other experimenters, Franklin made sparks from electrically charged Leyden jars and the sight of the spark and the tiny crack it made reminded him of lightning. Could lightning be a giant electrical spark? Ben wondered. And if so, how could he prove it?

His first plan was to put a metal rod on top of a church steeple and draw off some of the electric charge from a thunder cloud. But the church steeple he had in mind hadn't been built and within a few months a French scientist followed Ben's plan and performed the test. It proved that lightning was indeed made of electricity – but it was really dangerous. If lightning hit the metal pole anyone close by would meet a shocking end. As Russian scientists Georg Richmann found out to his cost...

The St. Petersburg Times

RUSSIAN RICHMANN ROASTED!

by ace reporter Hall D. Frontpage

Top scientist Georg Richmann has been struck dead by lightning. The Russian boffin was seen rushing home to perform a dangerous experiment. Richmann, 42, wanted to measure the strength of the electric charge of a bolt of lightning. Today the Times talks to his long-time friend Mikhail Lomonosov.

"I tried to warn him. I said 'Georg, Franklin says electricity can jump from the lightning rod.' But did he listen? Silly idiot only put a metal ruler up close to the rod. He had a thread on the ruler and he wanted to measure how far the charge would lift the thread up.

"Yeah - it was a shocking error!

A giant spark shot out of the rod. It bounced off the ruler and struck Georg dead. I was thunderstruck! So was Georg and well, when I saw what the bolt had done to Georg, I bolted too. A pretty sight it was not."

Scorched shape in carpet shocks servants

By that time, Benjamin Franklin had conducted his own experiment on lightning. Of course, it was extremely dangerous, as you've just discovered. So did Ben share Richmann's fate and end up a fried Franklin-furter?

BENJAMIN FRANKLIN'S NOTEBOOK

1 October 1752

Dark overcast day,
really thundery, looks
like rain. Great! It's
ideal weather for my
kite flying test. I've
made a special kite
from an old silk
handkerchief.

HANDKERCHIEF
(BIT OF DRIED SNOT)

STRING
WITH
KEY
ON
THE
END

METAL SPIKE
TIED TO
KITE

SILK
THREAD
(SILK CAN'T
CARRY AN
ELECTRICAL
CHARGE)

My plan is to fly the kite in a thunderstorm
and pick up some electricity from the
clouds, which will run down the string and
charge up the key. But will it work? It's
not the danger of getting killed
that bothers me - it's getting
killed in public. I think I'd die
of embarrassment. So it's just
me and my son and we're going to a nice
quiet field where no one can see us.

Three hours later. . .

This is really frustrating. There's
no decent thunderclouds blowing
our way - my lad's really bored.
Oh well, better give up. No -
hold on, here comes one.

72

Now to get this kite in the air!
Wow! The threads on the string are standing on end – I figure they're electrified. I'm electrified too – with excitement. Let's put my hand near that key – better not touch it – OUCH!!! I got a painful electric shock. I'm so happy YES! YES! YES! Let's put a Leyden jar up to the key. There's a spark jumping into the jar – it's the static electricity I've been studying. Well that proves it. I've managed to draw electricity from the clouds and I'm still alive!

HORRIBLE HEALTH WARNING!

Franklin and his son were dead lucky – but they could have been unlucky and dead. If the kite had been struck by lightning then Ben would have been a has-Ben sorry, a has-been. Don't ever, EVER fly a kite in a thunderstorm or near high-voltage power lines.

Following this success Ben was soon hard at work designing an invention that would prevent lightning from striking your house and giving the cat a nervous breakdown.

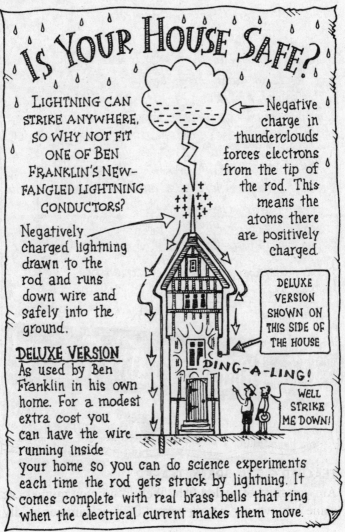

IS YOUR HOUSE SAFE?

LIGHTNING CAN STRIKE ANYWHERE, SO WHY NOT FIT ONE OF BEN FRANKLIN'S NEW-FANGLED LIGHTNING CONDUCTORS?

Negative charge in thunderclouds forces electrons from the tip of the rod. This means the atoms there are positively charged.

Negatively charged lightning drawn to the rod and runs down wire and safely into the ground.

DELUXE VERSION SHOWN ON THIS SIDE OF THE HOUSE

DELUXE VERSION
As used by Ben Franklin in his own home. For a modest extra cost you can have the wire running inside your home so you can do science experiments each time the rod gets struck by lightning. It comes complete with real brass bells that ring when the electrical current makes them move.

DING-A-LING!

WELL STRIKE ME DOWN!

Ben's discoveries made him famous. In those days North America was ruled by Britain but in 1776 Ben helped write the American Declaration of Independence. (It's said his co-authors had to keep an eye on Ben to stop him putting in silly jokes.) Ben became America's ambassador in France and won French support for the new nation.

Now back to lightning...

Bet you never knew!

In Victorian times some people carried lightning conductors on the end of their umbrellas. The device consisted of a metal rod on the spike of the umbrella, with a metal wire attached down which the lightning would run (and hopefully away from the petrified person holding the brolly). It worked in the same way as a full-sized conductor and was designed to keep its owner safe in a storm. But was this a smart idea? I mean, these umbrellas attracted lightning – would you put up with one?

WARNING!
PURCHASERS WERE ADVISED NOT TO USE THE METAL WIRE TO WALK THE DOG

TEACHER'S TEA-BREAK TEASER

Are you fond of boiled fish? Well, if not you might have some left over from your school dinner. Hammer boldly on the staffroom door. When it squeaks open, smile sweetly, and shove the revolting fish dish under your teacher's nose saying...

I WAS JUST WONDERING IF THIS IS WHAT HAPPENS TO A FISH IF THE SEA IS STRUCK BY LIGHTNING?

Answer: It depends on how close the fish was. As you know, electricity can travel though water. Any fish close to the strike would get a massive electric shock and the heat from the strike would probably boil it too. The heat turns the water to steam and makes an explosion that can be heard underwater for many kilometres. Any divers close by would probably be deafened.

BOOM! COD HELP US!

LIGHTNING ADDITION QUIZ

This quiz is really easy. In fact, you can probably go through it like greased lightning, ha ha. All you have to do is to add up the numbers.

1) How many times does lightning strike somewhere in the world in a second? The answer = 14 + 86

2) What is the record number of times a person has been struck by lightning? The answer = answer **1)** – 93

3) Lightning is hotter than the surface of the sun. By how many times? The answer = answer **2)** – 1.5

4) In 1995 lightning struck a football match. How many were blasted by a single bolt? The answer = answer **3)** + 11.5

Answers:

1) 100. Luckily it isn't the same spot – after all, lightning never strikes twice in the same place, so they say. Mind you, some people do seem to get more than their fair share of lightning strikes…

2) 7. US park ranger Roy Sullivan was struck *seven* times. That's at seven *different* times – not all on the same day. That really would have put him off his tea. In 1942 he lost his toenail (he must have been cut to the quick); in 1969 his eyebrows were burnt off; the following year his shoulder was burnt; in 1972 and 1973 his hair caught fire – "hair we go again", as he might have said; in 1976 his ankle was injured; and in 1977 his chest was burnt ... but I expect he was getting used to it by then.

3) 5.5. Lightning can be 30,000°C (54,000° F) and the surface of the sun is a rather tepid 5,530° C (9,980° F). No wonder a lightning strike can melt solid rock – and that's not your auntie's rock cakes we're talking about here. (They'd probably survive intact.)

4) 17. The victims were all parents and children from Kent, England. They all survived, but some of them suffered nasty burns.

Now, how about poor old Andy Mann – is he badly burned too? Is he *still alive*? Let's grab a bunch of grapes and rush over to the hospital.

A CHECK ON ANDY MANN

The good news is that Andy is sitting up in his hospital bed and watching the darts final on TV. The bad news is that he's suffered a few injuries.

PATIENT RECORD

NAME: Andy Mann   **Age:** 35

GENERAL NOTE: This patient has a severe attitude problem. He has been complaining loudly about a Professor Buzzoff.

SYMPTOMS: The patient shows signs of having been struck by lightning.

1 There are burn holes in his clothes and his sideburns are frazzled.

2 A leaf-like pattern of dead flesh on his skin shows where the lightning has burnt through it.

3 Since it's easier for the lightning to run over his body than to push through his skin and enter his body, this is what happened. Bleeding between his toes shows where the electricity left his skin and entered the ground.

Although the lightning was hot enough to kill him, as is common in a lightning strike, it didn't stay long enough to do fatal damage.

FORCED AIR

CLONK!

4 The patient was knocked out for about a minute. This was caused by the force of air pushed ahead of the lightning bolt. He was lucky not to suffer broken bones.

<u>PROGNOSIS</u>: If the lightning had actually gone through the patient's body the shock of being struck by lightning might have made his heart stop and resulted in death. As it is – he's lucky to be alive but should make a full recovery.

HUH ~ ME LUCKY? ME BOILERSUIT'S RUINED, ME EARRING'S MELTED, AND THERE'S AN OLE IN ME 'AT. AND I BET ME SIDEBURNS WON'T GROW BACK NEITHER. TELL THE PROF I WANT DAMAGES AND DANGER MONEY!

So you've been warned. Electricity can do shocking things to the human body. Oh, so you want to know more? Well, if you want to check out the gruesome details you can – just carry on reading...

SHOCK TREATMENT

Getting a massive surge of electricity running through your body is no picnic, as we've seen, but that didn't stop certain doctors using electricity to help people get better. Are you shocked? You will be. We'll be back after the commercial break...

ELECTRIC ADVERTS

Under the weather?

Enjoy a relaxing bath in real milk and then some electric shocks whilst sitting on a magnetic chair. You'll be buzzing with good health!

THE SMALL PRINT: This useless treatment was offered by Scottish doctor James Graham in 1774. Graham eventually lost all his money and went insane.

Hmm! Delicious milk!

THE SMALL PRINT: This useless bit of equipment was banned in the US because it gave the patient dangerous electric shocks. The advert should have said 'goodbye to melting patients'.

Goodbye to aching joints!

Simply strap an inductoscope to your affected region. Link the metal rings to a power point and watch your pain melt away.

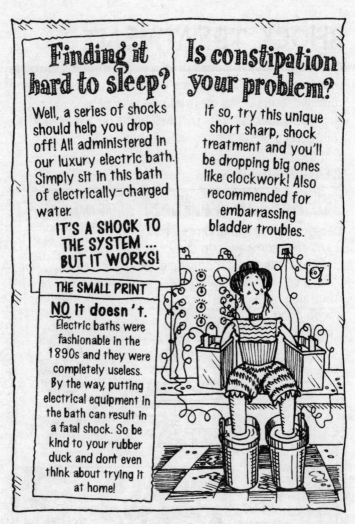

Finding it hard to sleep?

Well, a series of shocks should help you drop off! All administered in our luxury electric bath. Simply sit in this bath of electrically-charged water.

IT'S A SHOCK TO THE SYSTEM ... BUT IT WORKS!

THE SMALL PRINT

<u>NO</u> it doesn't. Electric baths were fashionable in the 1890s and they were completely useless. By the way, putting electrical equipment in the bath can result in a fatal shock. So be kind to your rubber duck and dont even think about trying it at home!

Is constipation your problem?

If so, try this unique short sharp, shock treatment and you'll be dropping big ones like clockwork! Also recommended for embarrassing bladder troubles.

Although it was about as useful as a pair of exploding underpants, all this primitive electric medicine is quite understandable, seeing as there is so much electricity in your body.

Oh yes there is...

Shocking electricity fact file

NAME : Electricity in the body

THE BASIC FACTS : **1** Your body contains enough electricity to light the fairy lights on a Christmas tree. No, DON'T wire your little brother/sister to the lights and check this detail. The electricity is found mainly in the nerves.

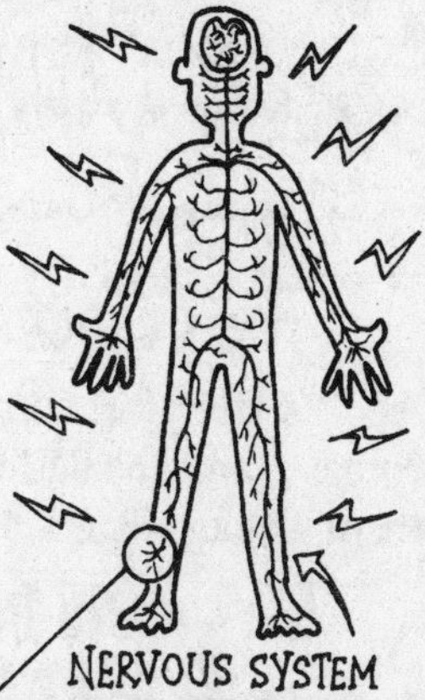

2 A nerve signal is made by positively charged atoms that flood into the nerve.

NERVOUS SYSTEM

NERVE SIGNAL

THE SHOCKING DETAILS:
Some animals sense electric forces. And some people and animals have much more than their fair share of electricity.

HEY! YOU'VE GOT MORE THAN YOUR FAIR SHARE!

BATTERY

THIS IS NOTHING! READ ON AND YOU'LL BE REALLY SHOCKED...

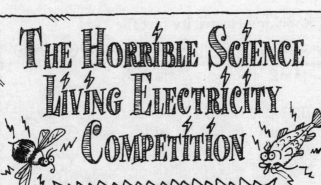

THE HORRIBLE SCIENCE
LIVING ELECTRICITY
COMPETITION

Class one - Nasty Nature

Yep, it's true that some animals can sense electrical forces - and the bad news is that this can make them vicious. Here are the most horrible examples...

3rd Prize:
HAMMERHEAD SHARK

3rd

Lives: Warm oceans

Sharks like the hammerhead can sense the electrical pulses in the nerves of their victims. To do this the hammerhead uses senses in its oddly-shaped bonce. But the shark is too good at its work because it also senses the electrical waves given off by submarine microphone cables (used to listen out for other subs) and attacks them! With shocking results ... for the shark that is.

ERK!

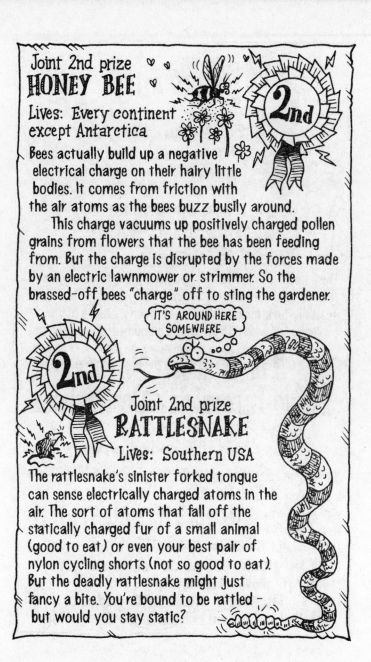

Joint 2nd prize
HONEY BEE

Lives: Every continent except Antarctica

Bees actually build up a negative electrical charge on their hairy little bodies. It comes from friction with the air atoms as the bees buzz busily around.

This charge vacuums up positively charged pollen grains from flowers that the bee has been feeding from. But the charge is disrupted by the forces made by an electric lawnmower or strimmer. So the brassed-off bees "charge" off to sting the gardener.

2nd

IT'S AROUND HERE SOMEWHERE

2nd

Joint 2nd prize
RATTLESNAKE

Lives: Southern USA

The rattlesnake's sinister forked tongue can sense electrically charged atoms in the air. The sort of atoms that fall off the statically charged fur of a small animal (good to eat) or even your best pair of nylon cycling shorts (not so good to eat). But the deadly rattlesnake might just fancy a bite. You're bound to be rattled – but would you stay static?

85

1st prize
FIRE ANTS

Live: Brazil and Southern USA

Fire ants sense electricity and they hate it (maybe they're just anti-social – ANTI-social, geddit?). What's certain is that the fearsome fire ants bite through wiring.

They confuse computers, pulverize plugs, terrorize traffic lights and mess up your microwave. Yes, they actually lurk inside microwave ovens, hiding in the cooler areas when it's on, only to pop out of your pizza!

THE HORRIBLE SCIENCE
LIVING ELECTRICITY COMPETITION

Class two – Shocking powers

3rd Prize
JAQUELINE PRIESTMAN

Lives: England, 1970s

(Note 99.9 per cent of humans don't have this power.)

Electricity: Jaqueline was studied by a scientist from Oxford University and found to have

ten times more electricity in her body than normal.

Shock value: Could make TVs change channels without touching them and power sockets explode. For some unknown reason she stopped being electric when she ate green vegetables. So greens really are good for you!

2nd Prize
ELECTRIC CATFISH

Lives: African rivers

Electricity: Makes 350 volts in a special muscle just under its skin. The electricity is made by moving positively charged atoms to one end of its body. This causes an electrical current in the same way that a movement of electrons in the same direction makes an electrical current (see page 141).

Shock value: Enough power to kill a fish but that didn't stop the ancient Egyptians eating it. Would you risk an electric shock from your supper?

THE TASTE IS SHOCKING!

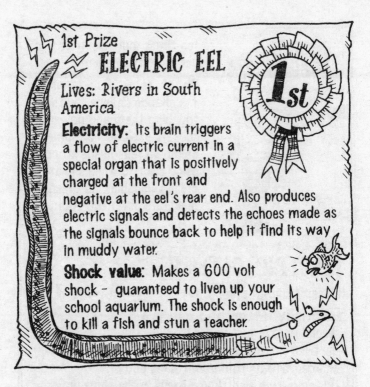

1st Prize

⚡ ELECTRIC EEL

Lives: Rivers in South America

1st

Electricity: Its brain triggers a flow of electric current in a special organ that is positively charged at the front and negative at the eel's rear end. Also produces electric signals and detects the echoes made as the signals bounce back to help it find its way in muddy water.

Shock value: Makes a 600 volt shock – guaranteed to liven up your school aquarium. The shock is enough to kill a fish and stun a teacher.

SOME SHOCKING FIRST AID

Imagine your teacher actually did suffer an electric shock. Would you know what to do? Well, you're about to find out...

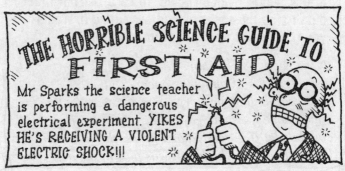

THE HORRIBLE SCIENCE GUIDE TO FIRST AID

Mr Sparks the science teacher is performing a dangerous electrical experiment. YIKES HE'S RECEIVING A VIOLENT ELECTRIC SHOCK!!!

Nasty! So what are you going to do to help? YES ... you've got to do *something*.

 GULP!

 CLICK!

1 Switch off the power. If you touch Mr Sparks before you do this you might get an electric shock too.

2 Even now don't touch Mr Sparks – you might still get a shock. Use a rubber or wooden object such as a ruler to knock away the electric wire.

3 Send someone to ring for an ambulance. Mr Sparks will need complete rest and a check-up. Oh well, looks like you can go home early from school. And having saved his life, chances are he'll be so grateful he'll let you off homework for the rest of term. Yeah right, dream on...

HURRY!

Bet you never knew!

If the victim is holding the electrified object the muscles of their hand will squeeze so they can't let it go. According to one story a pop star was holding his microphone when it gave him a severe shock. He couldn't let it go and ended up on the floor yelling loudly. Everyone thought it was part of the act!

HAVE A HEART

The most important electrical charge in your body is the signal (similar to a nerve signal) that controls your heart beat. It's made by an area of muscle in the upper part of the heart. The signal makes the heart muscle squeeze in a regular rhythm.

HOPE I DON'T HAVE A POWERCUT!

Each squeeze pumps blood into and out of the heart sending it around the body and keeping us alive.

The heart can be monitored using a brilliant gizmo called the electrocardiogram (e-leck-tro-car-de-a-gram) developed by Dutch scientist Willem Einthoven (1860–1927) in 1903. Metal electrodes on the chest pick up electrical pulses from the nerve signals that control the heart. The pulses pass along a wire stretched between the poles of a magnet, making the wire bend very slightly. The machine displays this bending as a pattern on a screen.

But if this rhythm ever breaks down it's SERIOUSLY BAD NEWS. The condition is called ventricular fibrillation (ven-tric-ular fib-brill-la-tion). The heart flutters helplessly like an injured bird and stops pumping blood. The blood brings life-giving oxygen (a gas taken from the air by the lungs) to the body and without it the body will die in minutes. *And the shocking truth is that this terrifying condition can be triggered by an electric shock.*

Bet you never knew!
But the heart can be re-started. Incredibly, the best way is to give it an electric shock. Yes, you did read that right – another electric shock!

For reasons that scientists don't quite understand, the shock stops the fluttering of the heart so it can re-start itself. This fact was discovered in an especially tragic fashion. Read on for the heart-rending details...

STRAIGHT FROM THE HEART
Arizona, USA, 1947

"Here we have an interesting case. A 14-year-old male with a chest that hasn't grown properly for several years – making him unable to breathe normally. Am I going too fast?"

Top surgeon Claude Beck glanced at the medical students who were taking notes and, as usual, following his morning ward round like a flock of white-coated gulls after a fishing boat.

Beck had short greying hair, a square face, a square jaw and looked you squarely in the eye even when he had bad news to announce. And right now he was gazing straight into the eyes of his young patient.

"I wish I could tell you the op will be a cinch son, but it's an involved procedure. We've got to separate your ribs from your breastbone so you can breathe normally. Still I reckon we'll pull it off." Mickey's eyes were huge and dark and the rest of him looked thin and pale under his crew cut.

"And then?" he whispered anxiously.

"You'll be right as rain."

Mickey struggled to ask another question but he was short of breath and the surgeon and his students had already moved on. So later he asked a nurse about Dr Beck.

"Oh yes, Mickey," she smiled. "He's a real expert. Why, he's so clever he's even gone and developed a machine to re-start hearts using electric shocks. It's called a defibrillator. He's been testing it out on dogs. So don't you worry – you're in good hands."

Beck did indeed pull it off. The operation went just fine and after two hours the ribs were separated. The tricky part was over and the surgeon sighed with relief as he carefully sewed up the wound. Then, without warning Mickey's heart stopped beating. The unconscious boy gave a gentle sigh as his life ebbed away.

There was no time to think – and only seconds to act.

"Cardiac arrest!" yelled Beck, grabbing a scalpel and slicing through the stitches holding the side of the wound. There was just one thing he could do, one terrible option. He pulled aside the bone and muscle and grabbed the boy's heart. It was quivering like a hot bloody jelly.

"Ventricular fibrillation!" he snapped. Already he was gently squeezing the heart in his hands – willing it to start pumping blood on its own. Willing the boy to come back to life. For 35 minutes the surgeon frantically massaged the heart between shots of drugs designed to stimulate the muscle – but he knew that he was only buying time. There was just one hope.

"Fetch my defibrillator!" he ordered. "I'm going to try to shock the heart."

He glanced at the white, strained face of the anaesthetist. She was shaking her head.

"But," she protested. "It's never been tested on humans – only dogs."

"We've got to try it," said Beck desperately. "If not..."

The porter quickly wheeled Beck's machine, a mass of wires and dials, into the operating theatre and plugged it into the mains.

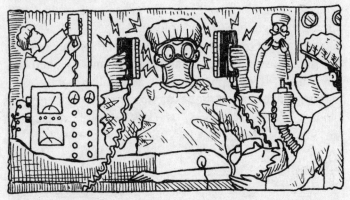

Beck placed the silver electric paddles to the boy's heart and fired 1,000 volts of electricity. The paddles jumped under Beck's hands but the heart was still, lifeless.

"We're losing him!" shouted the nurse.

Sweat ran down Beck's forehead and into his surgical mask. Once more he was frantically squeezing the slippery heart in his hands. Twenty-five agonising minutes passed, Beck's arms were aching but he dared not stop. More drugs were injected but still the heart would not beat. Perhaps it would be easier to let the boy die, Beck reasoned, knowing he could easily stop. But something drove him on.

"I'll try again," said the surgeon grimly, applying the paddles to the heart with shaking hands. Another jolt of electricity, longer this time, and 1,500 volts made the paddles jump.

There was a long tense silence.

"It's working!" said Beck, his voice hoarse with relief. The heart was pulsing and beating blood strongly and normally as if nothing had happened. And the nurses, the anaesthetist, the whole theatre staff broke into wild cheering.

Later that day Mickey was sitting up in bed.

"I'm starving," he complained. "The food here is shocking."

The nurse smiled, her eyes glistening with happiness and relief. "Well, Mickey," she said, "I think I can safely say we've all had a shocking time."

SHOCKING MEDICINE

1 Beck's defibrillator became a standard item of equipment in hospitals where it has saved tens of thousands of lives. Then, in 1960 US doctors developed a battery-powered version that could be used in ambulances. And today there are even small defibrillators that can be implanted inside the body. These fire tiny jolts of electricity into the heart if its rhythm breaks down.

2 The pacemaker is a similar device. Like an implanted defibrillator it runs off a battery outside the body but

unlike a defibrillator it produces regular shocks to keep the heart beating normally. In 1999 surgeons implanted a tiny pacemaker – the size of a 50 pence coin – to boost the heart of a three-week-old baby.

HIS NAPPY NEEDS CHANGING EVERY DAY BUT NOT HIS BATTERIES

PACEMAKER

3 In 1995 surgeons equipped a British woman with a battery-operated machine that helped her stand up. The woman's nerves had been damaged in a car accident and the machine fired electrical signals to her undamaged nerves to make her muscles move.

Have you spotted what these inventions have in common? No? Well, here's a clue – it's metal, it's full of chemicals and produces energy. No – it's not a can of fizzy drink! It's a battery, and without it most machines would be so much scrap metal. Well, by some shocking coincidence the next chapter's all about batteries – so why not read on? You can stretch yourself on the sofa and relax as you read. It's sure to re-charge your batteries – ha ha.

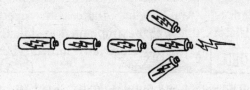

BULGING BATTERIES

Remember those kids on the Island of Horra? Bet they wished they'd brought a few batteries with them! Batteries are a great way of storing electricity so you take it with you and use it to power torches and radios and toy cars and walking, talking, crying, peeing dolls ... whatever you want. But how do they work?

TEACHER'S TEA-BREAK TEASER

All you need is a battery and a big grin. Knock on the staffroom door and when it creaks open hold up the battery.

Your teacher will probably say "It's a battery you little idiot!" Then you can shake your head sadly.

Yes, the correct name for a "battery" is a "dry cell". It's called that because the chemicals inside are in a paste and

97

not in a liquid as they were in the first batteries, or cells. The word "battery" actually means a number of cells put together to make power, as in a torch. Anyway, we'll go on using "battery" in its everyday sense.

Shocking electricity fact file

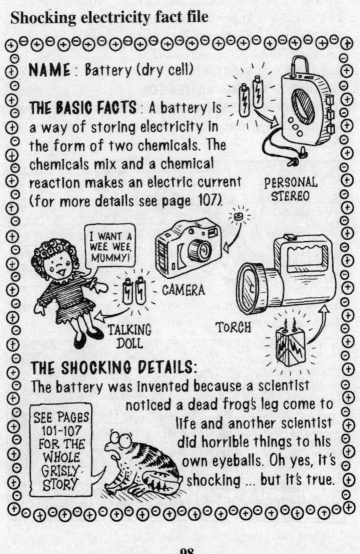

NAME: Battery (dry cell)

THE BASIC FACTS: A battery is a way of storing electricity in the form of two chemicals. The chemicals mix and a chemical reaction makes an electric current (for more details see page 107).

PERSONAL STEREO

I WANT A WEE WEE, MUMMY!

CAMERA

TALKING DOLL

TORCH

THE SHOCKING DETAILS:
The battery was invented because a scientist noticed a dead frog's leg come to life and another scientist did horrible things to his own eyeballs. Oh yes, it's shocking ... but it's true.

SEE PAGES 101-107 FOR THE WHOLE GRISLY STORY

Hall of Fame: Luigi Galvani (1737–1798) and Alessandro Volta (1745–1827) Nationality: Italian

This is the story of two Italian scientists who started off as friends and ended up deadly enemies, and on the way both made major contributions to the science of electricity.

ALESSANDRO'S STORY...

The clever boy was educated by priests. His teachers were so impressed by him they tried to bribe him to train as a priest by giving him sweets.

But Alessandro's family didn't want their son to be a priest and took him away from school. (If only all families were so understanding!) Young Alessandro became interested in science and became a science teacher at Como and later a professor at Pavia University.

Alessandro got interested in electricity when he invented a pistol fired by an electric spark produced by static electricity. This set fire to methane gas contained in the pistol. Remember methane – it's the gas found in farts and rotting rubbish. And no, before you ask, you can't use exploding farts to shoot people.

Luigi's story

Young Galvani trained to be a doctor and later lectured in medicine at the University of Bologna whilst working as a doctor. He made a study of bones and later kidneys without making any startling discoveries.

But in the 1780s he became interested in nerves and made an electrifying breakthrough. Anyway, here are the letters that Luigi and his buddy Alessandro wrote to one another (beware, they could well be forgeries).

Bologna University 1780

MY METAL SCALPEL

Dear Aless,
You'll never guess what's happened! I was cutting up a frog's leg - as you know I'm researching nerves - and something shocking happened. There was a spark and the frog's leg twitched!

FROG'S LEG

METAL SHEET UNDERNEATH

Well, I checked and the frog was definitely dead. Oddly enough, the leg only seems to twitch if you touch it with metals. Bone or glass, for example, don't work. So I tried an experiment - I fixed some frog legs with brass hooks to the iron bars outside my lab windows and get this! The legs were all twitching merrily like a line of high-kicking dancers. The neighbour's cat got a real shock!

I think the frog's muscle contains electricity which forms a current through the metal. I think this electricity is the spark of life itself -

already some of my fellow scientists are trying to bring dead bodies back to life by giving them electric shocks – no success there I'm afraid! But I'm still really excited – in fact I'm galvanized. Nice word that!*

Your mate, Luigi

Dear Luigi

That's a really interesting discovery but I'm sorry to say I don't think you're right about electricity in the body. First of all I gave an electric shock to a live frog. The frog trembled but it didn't jump. "Why not?" I asked myself. I decided to investigate whether electricity makes our senses work. So I gave my tongue and eyeballs and ears electric shocks to see if I started tasting, seeing and hearing things that weren't there. I didn't – and yeouch, it hurt!

Then suddenly I realized the shocking truth. I reckon it's the metals you used that made the electric current and it simply ran through the frog's leg and made it twitch. Since then I've actually managed to make electricity flow between two metals like this...

ONE BOWL CONTAINS A BAR OF ZINC

BARS LINKED BY WIRE. IF YOU TOUCH THE WIRE YOU GET AN ELECTRIC SHOCK.

ONE BOWL CONTAINS A BAR OF COPPER

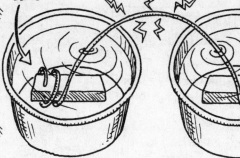

TWO BOWLS OF SALTY WATER (I HAVE FOUND BY EXPERIMENT THAT THE ELECTRIC CURRENT TRAVELS MORE EASILY THROUGH SALTY WATER.)

So there you have it...
Your pal,
Alessandro →

SCIENTIFIC NOTE

1 Volta was right. Like any animal or human body the frog's leg was mostly salty water and electricity can travel through this mixture. But Galvani wasn't totally wrong – after all, the nerves do send a kind of electrical signal (check back to page 83 if you're not sure what I'm talking about).

2 Volta was right about his experiment too. Electrons flow from the zinc to the copper and this forms an electric current. But Galvani wasn't impressed.

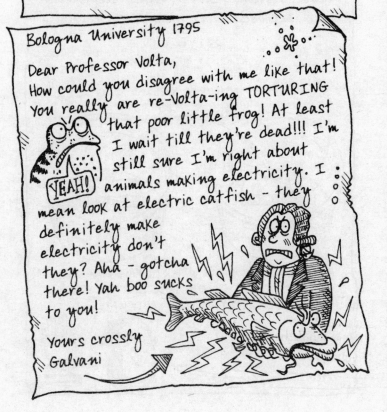

Bologna University 1795

Dear Professor Volta,
How could you disagree with me like that! You really are re-Volta-ing TORTURING that poor little frog! At least I wait till they're dead!!! I'm still sure I'm right about animals making electricity. I mean look at electric catfish – they definitely make electricity don't they? Aha - gotcha there! Yah boo sucks to you!

Yours crossly
Galvani

YEAH!

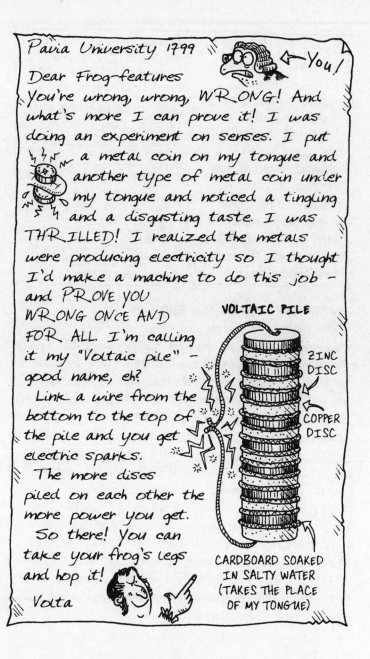

Pavia University 1799

← You!

Dear Frog-features

You're wrong, wrong, WRONG! And what's more I can prove it! I was doing an experiment on senses. I put a metal coin on my tongue and another type of metal coin under my tongue and noticed a tingling and a disgusting taste. I was THRILLED! I realized the metals were producing electricity so I thought I'd make a machine to do this job – and PROVE YOU WRONG ONCE AND FOR ALL. I'm calling it my "Voltaic pile" – good name, eh?

Link a wire from the bottom to the top of the pile and you get electric sparks.

The more discs piled on each other the more power you get.

So there! You can take your frog's legs and hop it!

Volta

VOLTAIC PILE

ZINC DISC

COPPER DISC

CARDBOARD SOAKED IN SALTY WATER (TAKES THE PLACE OF MY TONGUE)

WHAT HAPPENED IN THE END?

Galvani never gave up his idea and he never forgave Volta for disagreeing with him. He lost his job when the French Emperor Napoleon took over in Italy because he wouldn't support the French, and died a disappointed man. Volta got on well with the Emperor who made him a count and his invention made him famous. Today the volt, a unit that measures the amount of "pressure" behind electrons in an electric current, is named after him.

Bet you never knew!
The problem with Volta's invention is that the soggy cardboard kept drying up. The more familiar battery of today (the dry cell – remember?) was invented in 1866 by French inventor Georges Leclanché (1839– 1882). It uses a mixture of chemicals to make chemical reactions that result in electrons flowing from the zinc inner container to the carbon rod.

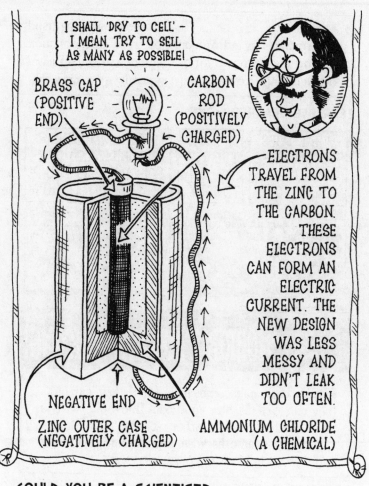

COULD YOU BE A SCIENTIST?

Which way round do the batteries go in a torch? Yeah, OK you can try it out – or you could think about which way the electrons move. Is it…

a) Positively charged end to positively charged end?

b) Negatively charged end to negatively charged end?

c) Negatively charged end to positively charged end?

Answer: c) Remember that negative electrons flow towards positive atoms – so for electricity to flow and your torch to work you have to put the negative and positive ends together.

TERRIBLE TEACHER JOKE

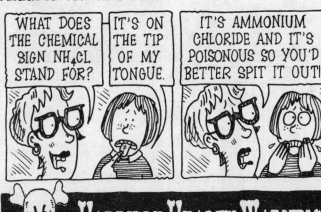

WHAT DOES THE CHEMICAL SIGN NH4CL STAND FOR?

IT'S ON THE TIP OF MY TONGUE.

IT'S AMMONIUM CHLORIDE AND IT'S POISONOUS SO YOU'D BETTER SPIT IT OUT!

HORRIBLE HEALTH WARNING!

Battery chemicals can be harmful. If they leak out they can even dissolve your skin! Throw old batteries away (and not in the fire) or recharge them. Never try cutting one open otherwise your burning curiosity might result in burns in your underwear.

BRILLIANT BATTERIES

The brilliant thing about batteries is that you can use them anywhere. On the beach and in the car and in the toilet. And there's plenty of choice of batteries each using different chemicals to produce electrons and make an electric current.

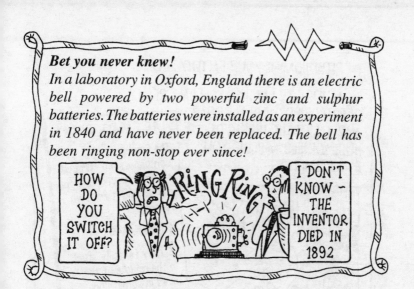

One of the most interesting battery-powered machines is the battery-powered car – no not a toy one, a real one. By the 2000s scientists were developing cool cars that could drive hundreds of km without a recharge. Japanese students even built one car that could zoom at 122 km (76 miles) per hour even though it was powered by ordinary AA batteries. Mind you, back in 1985 things were very different. A battery car was launched with massive hype. But was it more hype than horsepower?

SATISFY YOUR DRIVING AMBITION!

YOU DON'T NEED A DRIVING LICENCE TO OWN A SINCLAIR C5! INVENTED BY INVENTOR SIR CLIVE SINCLAIR, THIS BATTERY POWERED TRICYCLE CAN GO 32 KM WITHOUT BEING RECHARGED!

READ ON FOR MORE INFORMATION

➤ PEDAL HOME IF YOUR BATTERY FAILS!

➤ AT JUST 79 CM HIGH YOU CAN REALLY GET TO GRIPS WITH THE ROAD AND ENJOY THE THRILLS OF HUGE LORRIES MISSING YOU BY MILLIMETRES

THE SMALL PRINT

The Sinclair C5 company soon stopped trading. People were put off buying it for two reasons.

1 Safety fears.

2 They felt silly stuck in the middle of the road in something that looked like a kid's pedal car.

So there you have it, batteries are a great way to produce the electrical force to get things on the move. Even a Sinclair C5. But there's another kind of force too that's found in the C5's electric motors and indeed in any other electric motor.

And it's made by our old friends the electrons...

Wanna know more?

Well, read on, you're bound to feel drawn to the next chapter. It's mysteriously attractive ... just like a magnet!

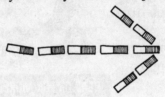

MYSTERIOUS MAGNETISM

Are you finding this book hard to put down? I expect it's the magnetic force coming from these pages. If you can *force* yourself to read the next few pages you'll find out what magnetism is and how it's made. Let's face a few facts...

Shocking electricity fact file

NAME: Magnetism

THE BASIC FACTS: **1** Magnetism is made by magnets. (Well, knock me over with a feather duster!)

2 *What we call magnetism is actually the same force as the electric force made by electrons –* that's why the posh scientific name for the force is electromagnetism (e-leck-tro-magnetism).

MAGNET

FORCE MADE BY ELECTRONS

REMEMBER THIS ON PAGE 41?

3 What this means is that every atom which has electrons is very slightly magnetic.

THE SHOCKING DETAILS:
QUESTION: But if atoms are magnetic and atoms are everywhere then how come everything isn't magnetic? How come you're not stuck to your bed in the morning? (No you're not, it just *feels* like you are.)

ANSWER: I said "slightly magnetic". You only notice a magnetic force if many billions of slightly magnetic atoms line up together.

MAGNETISM: THE INSIDE STORY

So how do you line up all those atoms? I mean, you'd need a tiny pair of tweezers and loads of patience and it would still take for ever.

THERE'S GOT TO BE AN EASIER WAY...

Well, you'll be pleased to know that inside a magnet this lining up is done quite naturally by those nice helpful atoms.

1 Inside a magnet the atoms line up to form little boxes (about 0.1mm across) called domains (doe-mains). Inside these boxes the electrons can combine their forces to make what we call a magnetic force.

2 A magnet has two ends called north and south poles.

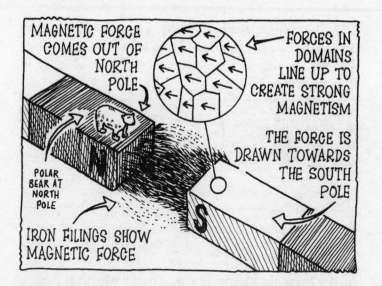

MAGNETIC FORCE COMES OUT OF NORTH POLE

FORCES IN DOMAINS LINE UP TO CREATE STRONG MAGNETISM

THE FORCE IS DRAWN TOWARDS THE SOUTH POLE

POLAR BEAR AT NORTH POLE

N

S

IRON FILINGS SHOW MAGNETIC FORCE

Dare you discover ... how to make a magnetic plane?

You will need:

A piece of tissue paper 2 cm x 1 cm

Sticky tape and scissors

A metal pin

A magnet (This should be as strong as possible – you could use several magnets in a line.)

A piece of thread 30 cm long.

What you do:

1 Thread the pin through the paper so it looks like a little plane (the paper being the wing).

2 Tie the string to the head of the pin.

3 Tape the end of the string to the side of a table.

4 Move the magnet near to the plane and try to make it fly without touching it.

What do you notice?

a) If I move the magnet away from the plane it stays flying.

b) The closer the magnet is to the plane the better it flies.

c) The magnet will only work if it's a certain way round.

Answer: b) The closer you are to the magnet the stronger its force. The area around a magnet that is affected by its force is called a "magnetic field". (Mind you, don't tread in any magnetic cow pats!)

Dare you discover ... if magnetism works underwater?

(No, you don't need a diving suit for this experiment.)

You will need:

A glass of water

A magnet

A paper clip

What you do:

1 Plop the paper clip in the water.

2 Place the magnet up against the *outside* of the glass.

3 Now try to use the magnet to bring the paper clip to the top of the glass without touching the paper clip and without getting the magnet wet.

GREAT
CONCENTRATION
IS REQUIRED

What do you notice?

a) It's easy.

b) I can't move the paper clip at all.

c) The paper clip only moves when I hold the magnet *over* the water. This proves that magnetism works through water but not through glass.

Answer: a) This proves that magnetism works through glass and water.

Dare you discover ... how magnetic tape works?

Did you know that tape recorders work using magnetism? Yes, it's true. To find out more try this fascinating experiment.

You will need:

A cassette tape

A cassette recorder and microphone

A magnet

What you do:

1 Talk into the microphone. No, it doesn't really matter what you say – why not try a few farmyard impressions?

2 OK, that's enough farmyard impressions – I said THAT'S ENOUGH FARMYARD IMPRESSIONS!

Now rewind and play the tape. Rewind the tape and stop in the middle of your recording.

3 Now sweep the magnet across the tape four times.

4 Rewind and play the tape.

What do you notice?

a) My voice blanks out in the middle. My lovely recording is ruined!

b) The tape is LOUDER than ever and all the neighbours are complaining.

c) My voice sounds like an alien's.

Answer: a) The microphone turns your voice into electronic pulses and these are turned by a magnet into magnetic signals that rearrange the tiny bits of metal chemical on the tape to make a recording. Easy-peasey! Your magnet muddled up these chemicals so that the tape recording was lost.

116

HORRIBLE HEALTH WARNING!

Don't you DARE even *think* of using your mum and dad's classic tape collection for this experiment! Oh I see, it's too late. Well beware – your parents might use a magnet to grab your pocket money.

MAGNETIC QUIZ

1 Some Canadian coins are magnetic. TRUE/FALSE

2 Magnetism can be used to suck out diseased parts of bone marrow (the juicy pink bit that dogs love). TRUE/FALSE

3 An ultra-powerful magnet can pull the eyeballs out of your head. TRUE/FALSE

4 Magnetism stores information in computers. TRUE/FALSE

5 In Siberia people fish by chucking iron filings into lakes. When the fish have eaten the filings they are caught using magnets. TRUE/FALSE

6 There's a magnet inside your school bell and/or your school fire bell. TRUE/FALSE

7 Magnetism can power a full-sized train. TRUE/FALSE

Answers:

1 True. Canadian dimes are made of nickel – a metal that can be naturally magnetic.

2 True. In the mid-1980s British scientists discovered how to treat lumps of diseased bone marrow inside bones with chemicals coated in magnetic material. The chemicals stuck to the affected areas inside the bone. It was then possible to draw the diseased lumps out in tiny bits using powerful magnets. Hungry yet, Fido?

3 False. Human eyeballs aren't magnetic but magnets *are* used to remove tiny bits of metal from eyeballs after accidents.

4 True. For example, a floppy disk stores computer code like a tape recording as magnetic chemicals on its surface. The "read" head of the computer turns magnetic pulses from the disk into electric signals inside the computer. The hard disk is a series of magnetic disks that store information.

5 False.

6 True. The ringing that wakes you up at the end of a science lesson is made by a hammer hitting a bell. The hammer is yanked by a powerful magnet in the bell that responds to an electric current set up when someone presses the button.

7 True. In the 1990s Maglev trains were built in Japan and Germany. The train is lifted off the rail using powerful magnets. As the train glides forward, powerful magnets on board make electrons move in the reaction rail underneath the train. This creates an electric current which gives off a magnetic force that pulls the train forward. Fancy one for Christmas?

Maglev technology has also been used to make lifts and some really cool theme park white knuckle rides. With a bit of luck you could persuade your parents to let you go on one for your science homework. Well, you can only ask.

A FORCEFUL TALE

Magnets have a long history. About 2500 BC, according to legend, a Chinese Emperor guided his army through fog using a rock containing magnetite (also called lodestone). Well, stone me. He probably used a sliver of the rock hung from a thread.

Magnetite is naturally magnetic so a sliver of it points towards the north and can be used to make a compass, a device described by Chinese scientist and astronomer Shen Kuo (1030–1093) in 1088.

Chinese sailors used the compass to steer a course at sea, a technique that spread to Europe and the Middle East within 100 years. But although sailors happily used compasses, no one bothered to do experiments with magnets until a doctor called William Gilbert (1540–1603) came on the scene.

WONDERING WILLIAM

Little is known about William's early life. But he studied medicine and eventually became Royal Doctor to Queen Elizabeth of England.

HOW IS YOUR ROYAL ILLNESS – I MEAN HIGHNESS?

But just two years later the Queen died, so William's medicines must have been a dead loss. Anyway, he was the first person to investigate magnets in a scientific way. For example, people thought that if you rubbed a magnet with garlic the pong would drive the magnetism away. (Sounds reasonable – after all it can have this effect on your friends.) But Gilbert found the treatment didn't work.

THIS EXPERIMENT STINKS!

MY RESULTS ARE NOT TO BE SNIFFED AT

Gilbert was fascinated by the way that a magnetic compass pointed north and wanted to know why. At last he realized that the whole Earth is a magnet! He found this out by putting a magnetic compass needle on a small rod. The needle pointed north of course but it also dipped slightly downwards. This suggested that magnetism must come out of the Earth at some point far to the north and Gilbert reckoned (rightly) that the Earth itself is a GIANT magnet. I guess that's one magnet that would be too big for your fridge.

FIVE MAGNETIC EARTH FACTS

1 A sea of melted metal surrounds the Earth's core. If you fancied a dip you'd be crushed and burnt – but fortunately no human has ventured this deep.

2 Currents swirl around in the metal and the huge masses of electrons set up powerful electric and magnetic forces.

3 The magnetic forces come out of the ground at the South Magnetic pole, sweep round the Earth and enter the ground at the North Magnetic Pole.

4 Yes, you did read that right – it's the *opposite* of an ordinary magnet! In line with other magnets we really ought to say that the North Magnetic Pole is near the South Pole and the South Magnetic Pole is near the North Pole – that would bamboozle your Geography teacher! The reason for the confusion is that the north pole of a compass magnet happened to get its name because it points towards the North Magnetic Pole, which is towards the geographic south. Lost yet? You will be.

SOUTH POLE BASE TO EXPEDITION – WHERE ARE YOU?

ER, HANG ON, WE'RE JUST READING PAGES 121 AND 122 OF SHOCKING ELECTRICITY!

5 The direction of the magnetic force has flipped round about 300 times in the last 4,600 million years. (Don't ask me why or when it will happen next – no one knows!) This would make a compass needle point south instead of north and if it happened on a school trip you're bound to get lost. And then your teacher would really flip!

Talking about expeditions – d'you fancy a holiday?

ENJOY A RELAXING BREAK WITH **MAGNET TOURS**

THE "OUT OF THIS WORLD" TOUR

Take a rocket to the fascinating Van Allen belts. No, these don't hold up Van Allen's trousers. Named after their discoverer James Van Allen, this region of radiation is affected by the Earth's magnetic force and extends over 128,000 km.

READ ON FOR DETAILS

Sun is like a big explosion firing out bits of atoms.

WOW! COR! FAB! COOL!

These bits are sucked into the Van Allen belts by the earth's magnetic force.

OUR SPACECRAFT

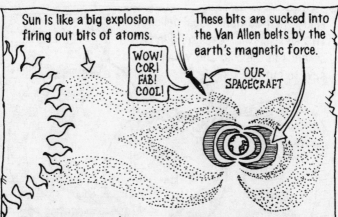

They hit atoms in the upper atmosphere which give out blips of light (photons) to make lovely displays of coloured lights. These are called the Northern and Southern lights because you can only see them near the north and south poles.

THE SMALL PRINT

SOMETIMES THE SUN FIRES VAST AMOUNTS OF EXTRA ELECTRONS. THEY SET OFF HUGE MAGNETIC WAVES IN THE VAN ALLEN BELTS THAT BOOST THE EARTH'S MAGNETIC FORCE. IF OUR METAL SPACECRAFT GETS CAUGHT IN ONE OF THESE SURGES YOU MIGHT FEEL SPACE SICK OR EVEN A BIT SPACED-OUT.

THE "SOUTH MAGNETIC POLE" TOUR

No, this isn't the actual South Pole (the base of the Earth) this is the place where magnetic forces actually come out of the ground. (Australian explorer Sir Douglas Mawson [1882-1958] was the first to get there in 1909.) You too will gasp in amazement as your compass needle wildly swings round.

TURN OVER FOR DETAILS

Sir D.M.

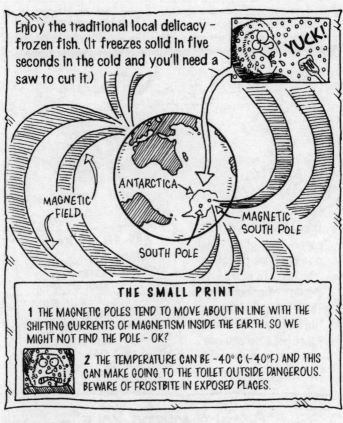

Enjoy the traditional local delicacy – frozen fish. (It freezes solid in five seconds in the cold and you'll need a saw to cut it.)

YUCK!

MAGNETIC FIELD

ANTARCTICA

MAGNETIC SOUTH POLE

SOUTH POLE

THE SMALL PRINT

1 THE MAGNETIC POLES TEND TO MOVE ABOUT IN LINE WITH THE SHIFTING CURRENTS OF MAGNETISM INSIDE THE EARTH. SO WE MIGHT NOT FIND THE POLE – OK?

2 THE TEMPERATURE CAN BE –40° C (–40°F) AND THIS CAN MAKE GOING TO THE TOILET OUTSIDE DANGEROUS. BEWARE OF FROSTBITE IN EXPOSED PLACES.

COULD YOU BE A SCIENTIST?

In 1995 American scientist Robert Beason stuck magnets to the heads of bobolinks (small American birds that normally fly south-east in the autumn). Beason then opened the birds' cages. What did the birds do?

a) Nothing. Their poor little magnetic heads were stuck to the metal floor of their cages.

b) They flew in roughly the right direction but they were slightly off course.

c) They flew in completely the wrong direction.

after-image.

Answer: c) Scientists think that birds have tiny specks of magnetite in their brains that act like compasses. With the added magnets mucking up their system, the bobolinks were well and truly lost. Birds such as brown pelicans have weaker magnets at the back of their eyeballs which affect the way that their eyeballs react to light to see colour. The pelicans can see the direction of magnetic north as a colour spot like an after-image.

Bet you never knew!
You can destroy the power of a magnet by "killing" it – that's the actual word scientists use. It sounds rather sinister, like some dreadful murder. Well, if it was a crime would you know how to solve it?

THE CASE OF THE MURDERED MAGNET...

THE CASE FILES OF OFFICER LODESTONE, NYPD.

Following a tip-off from some kids, we busted the flat of a science teacher. Judging by the still-warm cup of coffee he had only been gone a few minutes. The flat was a mess and I felt dirty just being there.

THE VICTIM

THE SUSPECT

The magnet was lying face down on the table.

CONTINUED...

125

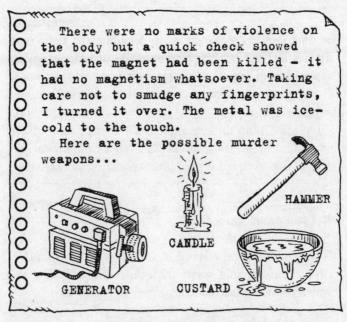

There were no marks of violence on the body but a quick check showed that the magnet had been killed — it had no magnetism whatsoever. Taking care not to smudge any fingerprints, I turned it over. The metal was ice-cold to the touch.

Here are the possible murder weapons...

GENERATOR

CANDLE

HAMMER

CUSTARD

Your mission ... is to find out how the magnet was killed. *Was it by...*

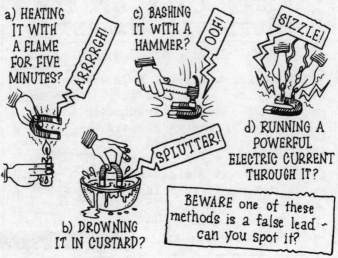

a) HEATING IT WITH A FLAME FOR FIVE MINUTES? ARRRRGH!

c) BASHING IT WITH A HAMMER? OOF!

SIZZLE!

d) RUNNING A POWERFUL ELECTRIC CURRENT THROUGH IT?

SPLUTTER!

b) DROWNING IT IN CUSTARD?

BEWARE one of these methods is a false lead — can you spot it?

Three of these methods would rearrange the atoms in the domains so the magnetic forces no longer pointed in a single direction. This would mean that the magnet lost its power. Read the case notes again ... you may find some more clues. OK – ready for this? The answer is **d)** and **b)** is useless!

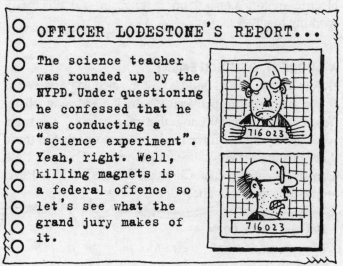

OFFICER LODESTONE'S REPORT...

The science teacher was rounded up by the NYPD. Under questioning he confessed that he was conducting a "science experiment". Yeah, right. Well, killing magnets is a federal offence so let's see what the grand jury makes of it.

716 023

716 023

What's that? Did you say "It doesn't sound too serious to me"? WELL, IT IS!!! You can't just go around killing magnets because magnets are vital and important. Vital to make THE MOST IMPORTANT MACHINE ON THE PLANET. A machine that literally powers the modern world. Wanna know more?

Well, why not "motor" on to the next chapter?

MIGHTY MAGNETIC MOTORS

Clean, silent, powerful. Electric motors power all sorts of things from washing machines to milk floats and the only time anyone notices them is when one doesn't work or gives their owners a nasty shock. But did you know that electric motors depend on magnetism and electricity working together?

A CURRENT OF EXCITEMENT

Before anyone could build a motor, scientists first had to figure out the link between electricity and magnetism. Yes, I know that you know that magnetism is the same force as the electric force made by electrons, but in those days electrons hadn't been discovered. Then in 1820 Danish scientist Hans Christian Oersted (1771–1851) stumbled across a connection.

Bet you never knew!
Christian's parents were too poor to feed their children so they gave Christian and his brother away to the neighbours. (No, your parents are unlikely to give your brother/sister to the folk next door so stop daydreaming and get on with this book.) But the boys managed to educate themselves from books. They did so well they were allowed into Copenhagen University, where Hans became a Professor.

Anyway, Hans wondered if an electric current had any effect on a compass needle. One day during a lecture he placed a compass needle near a fixed electric wire. The needle mysteriously swung away from the wire as if pushed by an invisible finger.

Oersted wasn't quite sure why this was happening but realized he'd stumbled across something really IMPORTANT.

COULD YOU BE A SCIENTIST?

You've been reading this book (unlike poor Oersted) so you can work out what was going on. What was it?

a) The electric force given out by the wire was pulling the magnetic compass needle towards it.

b) The force given out by the electrons in the wire was pushing the magnetic compass needle away.

c) The compass needle was moving as a result of static electricity.

Answer: b) The electric force is also a magnetic force – that's why it's called electromagnetism (remember that word from page 111?). And the forces made by electrons push against each other – remember that too? Well, the two forces pushed against each other as usual. This had the effect of pushing the compass needle away. (The wire would have moved too if it wasn't fixed.)

So the force from an electric current can make a magnet move and, as you're about to find out, this is exactly the principle behind an electric motor. Wanna know more?

Shocking electricity fact file

NAME: Electric motor

THE BASIC FACTS : **1** Every type of electric motor uses the electromagnetic force to make a wire loop move. Here's how...

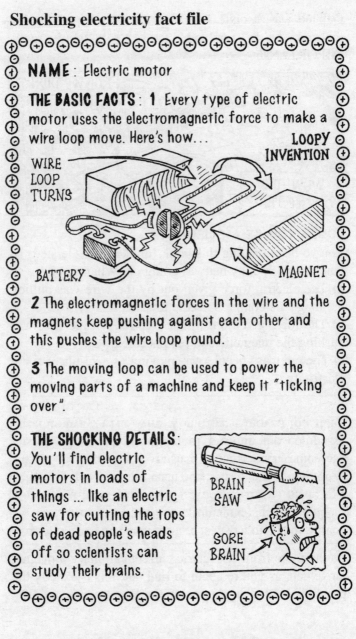

WIRE LOOP TURNS

LOOPY INVENTION

BATTERY

MAGNET

2 The electromagnetic forces in the wire and the magnets keep pushing against each other and this pushes the wire loop round.

3 The moving loop can be used to power the moving parts of a machine and keep it "ticking over".

THE SHOCKING DETAILS: You'll find electric motors in loads of things ... like an electric saw for cutting the tops of dead people's heads off so scientists can study their brains.

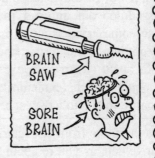

BRAIN SAW

SORE BRAIN

THE MOTOR RACE

The race was on to combine electricity and magnetism to make a working electric motor. But the basic idea was thought up in 1821 by scientist Michael Faraday (1791–1867). Faraday actually built a machine to show this and it was the first ever electric motor. In a first for *Horrible Science* we've actually persuaded the great scientist to explain how it works. (This is quite amazing since he's been dead for well over 100 years.)

DEAD BRAINY: MICHAEL FARADAY

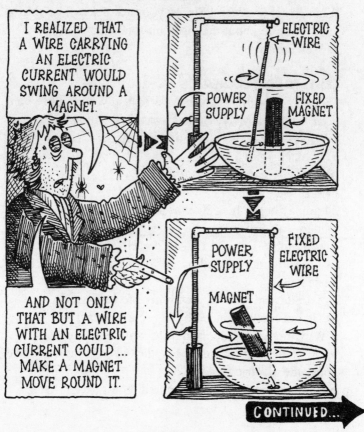

I REALIZED THAT A WIRE CARRYING AN ELECTRIC CURRENT WOULD SWING AROUND A MAGNET.

ELECTRIC WIRE
POWER SUPPLY
FIXED MAGNET

AND NOT ONLY THAT BUT A WIRE WITH AN ELECTRIC CURRENT COULD ... MAKE A MAGNET MOVE ROUND IT.

POWER SUPPLY
FIXED ELECTRIC WIRE
MAGNET

CONTINUED...

In each case the movement is due to the electromagnetic forces from the wire and magnet pushing against each other. Of course, if you touch the wire you'll get a nasty shock...

ARGH! I NEARLY KILLED MYSELF!

M.F. HAS FORGOTTEN THAT HE'S BEEN DEAD FOR OVER 100 YEARS

What an achievement! Surely your teacher will be able to tell you more about this brilliant scientist.

Well *surely*?

TEST YOUR TEACHER

Special note – this is a very easy test so you should award your teacher a MINUS mark for every *wrong* answer.

1 What did Faraday's dad do? Was he...

a) A blacksmith?

b) An ice-cream seller?

c) A science teacher?

2 Faraday began his career as a bookbinder's assistant but landed a job as lab assistant to top scientist Sir Humphry Davy (1778–1829). How did he do it?

a) Sir Humphry sacked one of his assistants and created a vacancy.

b) Faraday bribed Davy with his life savings.

c) He got recommended by his science teacher.

3 Why did Sir Humphry quarrel with Faraday?

a) Sir Humphry accused Faraday of stealing his ideas about the electric motor.

b) Faraday borrowed his pen and didn't give it back.

c) Sir Humphry was jealous because Faraday was a better teacher than he was.

4 What was Faraday's favourite hobby?

a) Work – especially setting up science experiments.

b) Going to parties.

c) Teaching children about science.

5 Other scientists made machines based on Faraday's work but found it hard to make them work. What did Faraday do?

a) Made copies of the machine and sent it to them.

b) Wrote them rude letters with the word IDIOT scrawled in big letters.

c) Organized a special training day for them.

6 As an old man what problem did Faraday suffer from?

a) A weak memory.

b) Embarrassing hairy ears.

c) He lost his voice so he had to give up teaching.

7 When the Chancellor of the Exchequer came to Faraday's lab and asked what use electricity was how did Faraday reply?

Answers: All the answers are **a)** so it should be easy enough to add up your teacher's score.

1 Faraday's dad was always ill and the family was very poor.

2 Faraday had already got a job as a secretary after giving Davy a beautiful handmade book of notes on Davy's lectures. Yes, producing marvellous homework does pay off sometimes.

3 Like many scientists Davy was very sensitive about who gets the glory for discoveries. Davy and his scientist pal William Hyde Wollaston (1766–1828) had worked on a motor that didn't work. Faraday had benefited from their ideas but hadn't mentioned them when he wrote about his discovery.

4 Faraday had few friends and no social life. But he wasn't sad – he was a genius. Obviously, your teacher has no such excuse. You can award half a mark for **c)** because Faraday enjoyed teaching at the Royal Institution where he worked and even set up Christmas lectures for children.

5 That's the kind of man he was.

6 This came after an illness in 1839 that Faraday said affected his head. It might have been poisoning by the chemicals he used for experiments.

7 And sure enough in 1994 the British government plonked Value Added Tax on electricity.

What your teacher's score means

-7–0 Your teacher's ignorance is SHOCKING. Order them to take the rest of the term off in study leave. Oh well, you'll just have to amuse yourself in science lessons.

1–3 Passable. Could do better.

4–7 Check your teacher's drawer for a copy of this book. If you find one disqualify your teacher AT ONCE! By the way, if your teacher keeps saying **c)** she is totally absorbed in her job and needs a nice long holiday. Of course, you'll have to take one too.

Bet you never knew!
All Faraday's motor did was run around in circles and not do any work. Do you know anyone like that? The first working electric motor was made by Joseph Henry (1797–1878) in 1831. Henry was another remarkable scientist. He started his career as a watchmaker and then wrote plays before getting interested in science. He was not a greedy man and when he got a science job working for the Smithsonian Institute he refused a pay rise for 32 years.

IF YOU DON'T STOP TRYING TO GIVE ME A PAY RISE...I'LL GO ON STRIKE!

Dare you discover ... how to make your own electric motor?

You will need:

A compass OR a needle

A magnet

A 25-cm length of thread

Some blu tak

Sticky tape

A 1.5-volt battery (HP11)

A piece of kitchen foil 28 cm x 6 cm

A grown-up to help. (Yes, they have their uses.)

What you do:

1 If you don't have a compass, stroke the needle with the magnet 30 times. This turns the needle into a magnet too.

2 Secure the needle to the end of the thread with a small blob of blutak in the middle so it hangs sideways in the air.

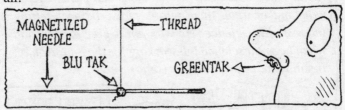

MAGNETIZED NEEDLE ←—THREAD

BLU TAK

GREENTAK ←

3 Stick the other end of the thread to a table top with more blu tak.

ANOTHER NUTTY EXPERIMENT!

BLUTAK

TABLE TOP

4 Fold the foil in half lengthways and then fold it again lengthways. Make sure you don't tear the foil.

5 Use sticky tape to stick one end of the foil to the positive end of the battery and the other end to the negative end. This makes a circuit for an electric current to run through.

6 Now, EITHER ... hold the battery horizontal and pass the foil loop from side to side over the face of the compass.

OR put the foil loop round the needle and move the foil up and down without touching it.

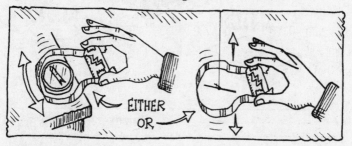

What do you notice?

a) The needle starts to glow with a strange blue light.

b) The needle twists round.

c) The needle jumps up and down.

Answer: b) The compass needle turns round and round and the needle twists around. Either way the magnetic field produced by the wire moves with the wire. This keeps pushing away and then attracting the magnetic needle – just like a real electric motor!

SPOT THE ELECTRIC MOTOR QUIZ

Which of the household objects on the next page contains an electric motor? (No, you're NOT allowed to take them apart to find out.) Here's a clue instead – if it's got moving parts it's got an electric motor.

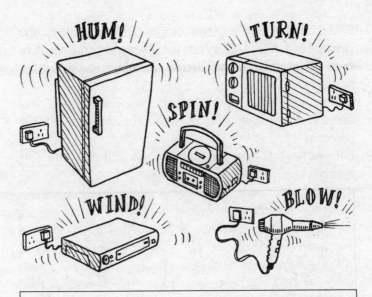

Answer: All of them!

Just take a look at this...

1 Ever wondered why fridges hum sometimes? (NO, it's not 'cos they're happy.) Specially cooled chemicals are pumped around pipes at the back that pass into the fridge and freezer areas.

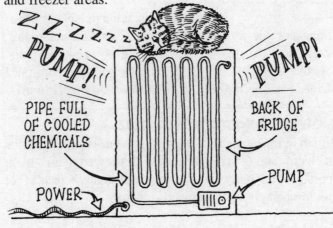

ZZZzzz
PUMP! PUMP!

PIPE FULL OF COOLED CHEMICALS

BACK OF FRIDGE

POWER

PUMP

2 In a microwave oven the food goes round on a turntable driven by an electric motor.

The motor also drives the fan that is used to reflect microwaves on to the food.

3 The CD player uses a laser beam to scan tiny pits on the underside of the CD. The laser beam jumps lightly as it scans the pits producing a reflected flickering pattern that the CD player turns into electric pulses that an amplifier can turn into sounds. Got all that? Well, the laser couldn't scan anything if the CD wasn't spinning and this is powered by an electric motor.

4 The DVD player is a bit like a CD player – only for sound AND images such as your favourite movies. Once again you need a electric motor to spin the disc so that it can be scanned by a laser beam.

5 A hairdryer is simply a coil of wire that heats up by friction as electrons crush through it (just like a light bulb – see page 21).

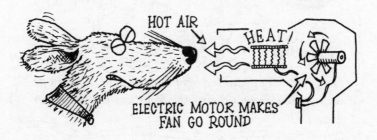

Mind you, an electric motor is pretty useless without an electric current to power it. And although you can make a current with a battery and some wire, if you want electricity on tap day and night you really need a more powerful current – so let's look at some shocking currents.

No, I mean *electric* currents... Amazingly enough, people have argued and died over the best way to make an electric current.

Bet you never knew!
Chances are you've actually generated your own electricity – if you own a bike dynamo, that is. The movement of your wheels makes a magnet go round. The magnet gives out a moving electromagnetic force that pushes electrons through the dynamo wire to light up your lamp.

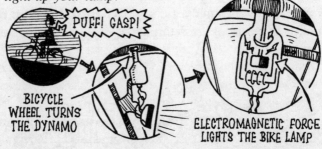

PUFF! GASP!

BICYCLE WHEEL TURNS THE DYNAMO

ELECTROMAGNETIC FORCE LIGHTS THE BIKE LAMP

The faster you pedal the brighter the light. Let's hope your penny-pinching parents don't use you to power their TV!

HIGH POWER - HIGH STAKES

Soon power generation became big business. And when electric power was launched in America in the 1880s the stakes were very high indeed. Leading the way were two power-hungry tycoons, Thomas Edison (1847–1931) and George Westinghouse (1846–1914).

Edison was a wealthy inventor with a multi-million-dollar power business complete with 121 power stations. He championed **direct current**, which means the electric current simply flows along a wire from the power station to your house. The problem was that the electrons gradually escaped through the wires so that the power stations had to be built quite close to houses and you needed one power station for each part of town.

George Westinghouse backed **alternating current**. The power station pumped out a current that kept changing direction. This made shock waves rush through the electrons in the wire at 300,000 kilometres (186,000 miles) a second. The advantage of this type of current was that it could be boosted using a device called a transformer and pumped into the wires at a massive 500,000 volts. And although electrons still leaked out of the wires there were more than enough to be carried long distances. At the other end of the wires a second transformer simply reduced the power to a safer level.

Westinghouse planned to take over Edison's business empire. But Edison insisted that alternating current was dangerous. Things were about to turn nasty ... shockingly nasty...

CRUEL CURRENTS

New York News
= August 1888

BAN THESE SHOCKING TESTS!

Professor HP Brown, a consultant hired by Edison, has been organizing shocking tests on cute fluffy animals to show the dangers of alternating current. The tests

HP Brown

involve shocking dogs and cats. When asked where he got the animals Brown turned red and said, "They just volunteered." He refused to say whether he's paid anyone for the animals.

142

STOP PRESS!

There have been a number of pet cats and dogs disappearing lately and the local kids seem to have more pocket money than usual.

NEW YORK NEWS

December 1888

A SHOCKING WAY TO GO!

New York State is to execute murderers. This follows embarrassing incidents when hangings have gone wrong and people have had their heads pulled off by the rope. The first victim to be

electrocuted is to be William Kemplar a fruitseller convicted of killing his girlfriend. Thomas Edison says the execution will prove the danger of alternating current.

W. Kemplar (before the murder)

⚡ STOP PRESS! ⚡

Westinghouse is shocked that his alternating current is going to be used to kill someone. Kemplar says he's shocked too and he's appealing, claiming the execution is too cruel. We expect him to be even more shocked if the execution goes ahead.

W. Kemplar (Yesterday)

NEW YORK NEWS

A DEAD LOSS

Kemplar is dead. His appeal was rejected after Thomas Edison claimed that electrocution wasn't such a bad way to go, because it kills nice and quickly. But the execution in the newly-designed electric chair went horribly wrong. Kemplar survived the first shock and took another jolt of over a minute resulting in smoke and sparks coming out of his body. The execution was a shocking sight

and a doctor present said: "I've heard smoking is bad for you but this is ridiculous!" before disappearing into the toilet.

WHAT HAPPENED NEXT?

Well, Westinghouse won. High voltage alternating current was the only way to move electricity any distance and in 1893 Westinghouse unveiled a powerful motor. It used alternating current and magnets that acted on first one side and then the other side of a metal loop. The motor was designed by a brilliant Croatian-born inventor named Nikola Tesla (1856–1943).

Some people thought Tesla was mad because he became a lonely old man who talked to the pigeons that lived in his New York apartment. Well, just imagine if one of the pigeon's had written Tesla's story. OK, I realize that's pretty unusual ... books by pigeons tend to be about flying.

TESLA AS I KNEW HIM...
By Percy Pigeon.

I like to think that Nikola and I were birds of a feather and yeah, sure he told me about his life – he was no bird-brain, let me tell you! Nikola was born in Croatia and his dad wanted him to be a priest but he wanted to be a scientist. So he talked his dad into letting him go to college. Mind you, he ruffled his teacher's feathers in a lesson on electric motors. Announced he could build a better electric motor – but no one believed him.

N. TESLA

Anyway, Nikola was in a park when he got the idea for this motor. He was reading poetry (why wasn't he feeding the pigeons?) and he drew the design on the ground with a stick. He built the machine the next year and soon after he went to America to work for this Edison guy. Nikola went there with four cents in his pocket, some plans for a flying machine he never got round to building, and his electric motor.

ELECTRIC MOTOR

But things didn't work out. Edison didn't like alternating current (whatever that is) which is how Nikola's machine worked, and he didn't like Nikola either. So, Nikola got himself hired by Edison's rival Westinghouse. He dreamt up a new transformer for making high voltages (whatever that is) and

TRANSFORMER

Westinghouse marketed the machine. Old Nikola was an amazing guy. His lab was full of giant lightning flashes given out by his high-voltage alternating currents. I reckon he was looking for a flash of inspiration.

Yeah, people say Nikola got weird. But all he said was he was in touch with aliens and that he'd invented a death-ray to shoot down planes. Sounds sensible to me! I mean planes are a menace to high flying pigeons. Anyway Nikola was my idea of a nice guy – generous with the breadcrumbs and he didn't even blow a fuse when I got my aim wrong and pooed on his head.

Time was when the electric motor was the height of high technology. But those were the days when even your most ancient teachers were still running around with squeaky little voices and teddy bears. Today we have electric machines that, although still powered by electric motors, can do a lot more than simply go round and round. Machines that calculate sums and help you play really cool high-tech computer games. Machines stuffed full of wonderful, interesting electronics. Devices that control the flow of electricity and make it do useful work.

So if you want to do some useful work take a look at the next chapter ... it's AWESOME.

AWESOME ELECTRONICS

Electronics is really about one thing. Getting electrons in an electronic current to perform fancy tricks inside machines by the use of clever gadgets and circuits.

CLEVER CIRCUITS

What is a circuit? Well, for an electrical current to flow it's got to have somewhere to flow to. A circuit is simply a wire arranged in a circle for the current to flow along and on the way there might be switches and bulbs and various electrical gadgets. Here's your chance to test your teacher's knowledge of circuits.

TEACHER'S TEA-BREAK TEASER

You will need a bird. No, not a real pigeon like Percy – a toy bird will do. All you do is tap gently on the staffroom door. When it opens, smile innocently and ask:

HOW COME BIRDS CAN PERCH ON A HIGH-VOLTAGE WIRE AND NOT GET ELECTROCUTED?

Answer: If the bird's going to get a nasty shock the electricity must flow through its body. But electricity must have somewhere else to go before it can flow – as in a circuit. So if Percy isn't touching the ground or a pylon at the same time as touching the wire he's safe.

CRUCIAL CIRCUIT TRAINING

To discover more about circuits, let's imagine a unique fitness centre, and remember those sparky electron kids from the Atom Family? Well, now they're being put through their paces by fearsome fitness fanatic, A Tomm.

THE ELECTRON FIZZICAL TRAINING CAMP

Crazy circuits

In our first event, the electrons race round a series of race tracks and light up bulbs and sound buzzers.

The first race is the series circuit – it's a nice, gentle warm up. The electrons must run from their battery hut round the wire, through the bulbs, and back to their battery. But so many electrons are crawling through the bulb wire that the rest get held up so they don't go too fast. A. Tomm isn't impressed.

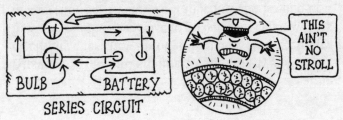

SERIES CIRCUIT

The second race is the parallel circuit. This is tougher and faster. A. Tomm has rearranged the wires so that there are two separate wires for each bulb. This means half the electrons can go one way and half can go the other so there's less of a bottleneck and the race is faster.

PARALLEL CIRCUIT

Super switches

Are you ready to make the switch? The electrons sure better be! In this exercise they'll have to get past the dreaded electrical switch. The switch is a springy piece of metal. When the switch is on the springy piece of metal is held down so the electrons crawling through the wire can crawl through it too. But they better be quick because when the switch is off the metal springs up and breaks the circuit. Leaving the electrons stranded!

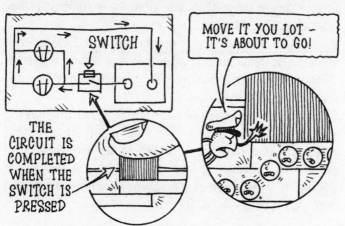

Fizzing fuses

Or should we call it frazzled fuses? In this heat (and boy, is it hot!) the electrons have to crawl though a narrow piece of wire. The resistance they get as they crawl through makes a lot of heat. If too many crawl in together the wire may melt so it's a real dangerous work-out.

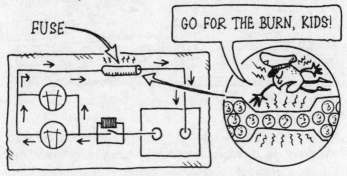

FUSE

GO FOR THE BURN, KIDS!

AND HERE ARE THE FULL FIZZICAL FACTS...

1 You get circuits everywhere electricity flows – so in your house a circuit runs round your light switches in each floor with separate circuits serving your power plugs. (Just imagine all those wires inside the walls!) As long as any of these switches is on, the current will flow. And that brings us to...

2 Switches. Besides power points you'll find switches in any electrical machine whether mains or battery operated. Well, how on Earth else are you going to turn it on – ask it nicely?

3 You get fuses in plugs and they're great for making sure too much current doesn't rush into an electrical machine. The number of amps in a fuse shows the amount of current it can take before it melts. Of course, if it did melt the machine wouldn't work and then you'd really blow a fuse!

HORRIBLE HEALTH WARNING!

That's why it really is a bad idea to use a single power socket to run your radio, TV, video and CD player on. The machines would use so much power that they'd melt the fuse!

SUPER SEMI-CONDUCTORS

From the 1950s onwards electronics was revolutionized by the invention of the semiconductor by a team of scientists led by William Shockley (1910–1989) working at Bell Laboratories, USA. A semiconductor isn't anything to do with a semi-detached house, a semicolon or a semicircle. It's actually two slices of an element (type of atom) called silicon – you can imagine it as a slice of holey Swiss cheese on a slice of bread.

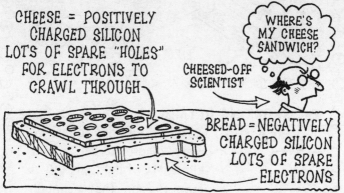

CHEESE = POSITIVELY CHARGED SILICON
LOTS OF SPARE "HOLES" FOR ELECTRONS TO CRAWL THROUGH

CHEESED-OFF SCIENTIST

WHERE'S MY CHEESE SANDWICH?

BREAD = NEGATIVELY CHARGED SILICON LOTS OF SPARE ELECTRONS

The electrons are quite happy crawling from the bread to the cheese but they can't return from the cheese to the bread. This means you can use a semi-conductor to control the direction that electrons flow. And then they can even be used to make power from the sun!

Shocking electricity fact file

NAME : Solar power

THE BASIC FACTS : A solar cell is simply that tasty cheese on bread semiconductor. Sunlight is made up of those tiny blips of light called photons.

1 Photons knock electrons in the bread free of their atoms.

2 Free electrons go off to explore the cheese.

3 More electrons move from the bread to take their place. This makes an electric current.

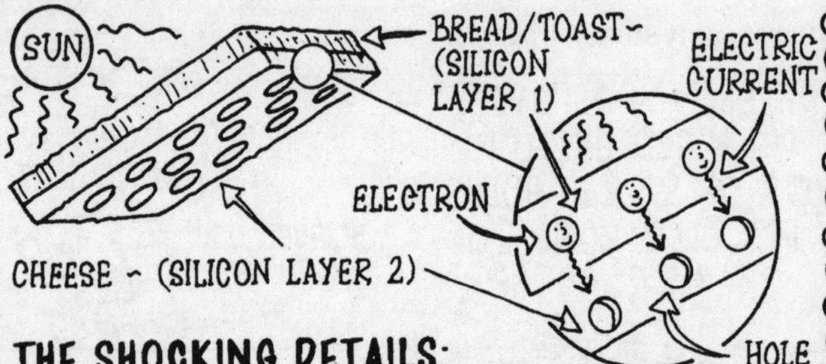

SUN

BREAD/TOAST~ (SILICON LAYER 1)

ELECTRIC CURRENT

ELECTRON

CHEESE ~ (SILICON LAYER 2)

HOLE

THE SHOCKING DETAILS:

In sunny parts of the world just one square metre of ground gets 2,000 kilowatts of light energy from the sun. That's enough to boil a kettle for six weeks. Mind you, if you did try that you'd boil the kettle dry before you got a cup of tea!

I'D RATHER HAVE A GLASS OF COLD WATER

SUPER SOLAR POWER

Amongst the uses found for solar power are a way to make power for spacecraft, experimental cars that can travel at 112 km per hour (70 miles per hour), and a solar-powered hat invented in 1967 by US inventor W Dahly. It used solar power to drive an electric fan hidden inside the hat to keep the wearer's head cool.

Sadly the invention proved a flop. I guess it didn't have too many fans.

Now back to semiconductors – did you know that without them a computer wouldn't work?

SUPER SILICON CHIPS

No, this is nothing to do with French fries. The chip is a semiconductor found in computers and many other gadgets. On its surface are hundreds and thousands of tiny switches called transistors. Each transistor is like a set of traffic lights at a road junction.

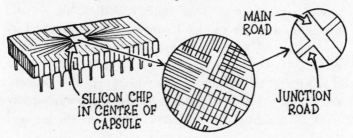

SILICON CHIP IN CENTRE OF CAPSULE

MAIN ROAD

JUNCTION ROAD

Electrons can only go along the "main road" if the current is also flowing for the "junction" road. By switching this "junction" current on and off very fast the transistor makes a current of one-off electrical pulses on the "main road" that make up basic computer code.

SILICON SECRETS

1 A silicon chip is made of silicon. (So how come you knew that already?) Anyway you can find silicon in sand. Yes, it's true, the insides of your computer probably started off loafing about on a beach somewhere.

2 Chips are shrinking. At the end of the 1960s the smallest silicon chip was 200,000 atoms across. By the end of the 1970s the smallest chip was 10,000 atoms across and by the end of the 1980s they were ten times smaller. And yet the finished chip is as complicated in its plan as a large city.

...3 BILLION DOLLARS TO DEVELOP THIS TINY CHIP, CARTER...AND YOU JUST DROPPED IT!!!!

Incredibly, it's now possible to make a chip a few dozen atoms across ... and in the future? Well, actually that's about as far as you can go. If you made a chip smaller its circuits would have corners too tight for electrons to flow round.

3 You might be wondering how you can get all that detail on a chip too tiny to hold. Actually, the boring fiddly work of adding the different types of silicon and aluminium to carry the current is done by robots. The only thing we humans need to worry about is getting dust or dandruff or dried snot in the chips and ruining them. (Of course robots don't have this problem.)

4 Nowadays silicon chips are found in loads of machines and not just computers. You can find silicon chips controlling DVD players and Play Stations, and Andy Mann's mobile phone and even walking, talking, peeing dolls. Yes – it really is chips with everything!

MIND YOU, IT STOPPED WORKING WHEN I DROPPED SALT AND VINEGAR ON IT!

There's a gap of 2,600 years between old Thales rubbing a lump of amber with a bit of fur to the latest up-to-the -minute silicon chips. Although it's a long time the vast leaps forward in technology are even more astonishing. But where's the tide of technology taking us? Are we heading for an electronic wonderland or could we slip back to the dark ages? What kind of shocks await us?

Better read on and find out...

THE FUTURE

EPILOGUE: A SHOCKING FUTURE?

In the olden days before electricity life was hard and cold and comfortless and slow. But that was then and today the world of electricity and electronics is buzzing with new ideas.

Some ideas are exciting, some are important and some are rather silly. Which ones do you think will take root, and which will quietly disappear like the solar-powered hat and the wobbling toilet seat? And what will they think of next? Let's switch on the TV.

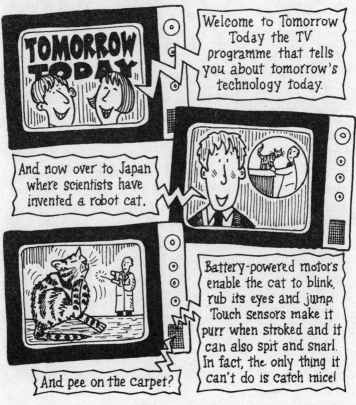

TOMORROW TODAY

Welcome to Tomorrow Today the TV programme that tells you about tomorrow's technology today.

And now over to Japan where scientists have invented a robot cat.

Battery-powered motors enable the cat to blink, rub its eyes and jump. Touch sensors make it purr when stroked and it can also spit and snarl. In fact, the only thing it can't do is catch mice!

And pee on the carpet?

Researchers from IBM have created a computer screen that gives you a picture as good as the very best TV. It works like the display of a calculator which uses liquid crystal blocks that give out light when an electric current runs across them.

The screen has no fewer than 5.5 million pixels (dots of light) powered by 15.7 transistors and 4.21 km of wiring.

Gosh!

That's nothing. A British university Professor has had a silicon chip-based control device implanted into his arm. The gadget switches on lights and computers without the professor having to touch them!

Any volunteers for this op?

And finally you can relax and unwind with a TV box. This nifty device turns a laptop computer into a TV and video recorder with full video editing facilities.

Besides new gadgets, scientists are working on longer-term research which might in time lead to new technology and more new gadgets. So what does the future hold? We've asked Tiddles the robot cat (alias Mystic Mog) to gaze into her mysteriously cloudy bowl of milk. Here's what she saw...

1 It's life ... but not as we know it

In 1952 Stanley Miller at the University of Chicago fired an electric spark through a mixture of gases. He was trying to copy the effect of lightning on gases in the air thousands of millions of years ago. His experiment had a remarkable result: amino acids – complex chemicals found in living things – formed from the gases. Scientists are still looking at ways in which electricity in the form of lightning may have given rise to life on Earth.

Prediction 1

Scientists find out how to make a new kind of life-form in a test tube using electricity and chemicals.

2 Powering ahead

Scientists in different parts of the world are developing plans to use the power of tides to make electricity. Although their plans vary they all depend on using the water rushing through narrow channels to drive turbines. In the 2000s other scientists were looking at building a huge chimney in the South African desert. Warmed by the hot sun, air will rise up the chimney and power generators to make electricity.

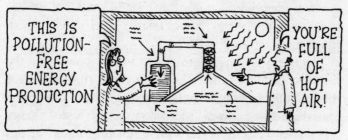

Prediction 2

One of these plans will come off and create a new technology which can make electricity for nothing *for ever.*

3 Real cool power

As long ago as 1911 Dutch scientist Heike Kamerliingh-Onnes (1853–1926) found that at very low temperatures, say just above -273° C (-459° F) metals like the mercury in a thermometer become superconductors. This means they lose their resistance to electricity – isn't that super! In 1957 a team led by US scientist John Bardeen (1908–1991) calculated that superconductor atoms wobble less when they are very cold allowing electrons to swim between the atoms without being knocked off course.

Prediction 3

Scientists invent a substance that allows electricity to run through it easily at room temperature. This opens the door to a new generation of electric machines that need scarcely any power to run.

Despite the promise of future progress most people still find electricity mysterious, but hopefully having read this book you won't be one of them. All most people know is that electricity is terribly useful and sometimes shockingly dangerous. But of course, electricity is much, much more.

Electricity is amazing. Amazing in its power and the limitless variety of the tasks that it can perform. And it's totally gobsmacking to think that the power behind this incredible force comes from astonishing blips of energy and matter – electrons and atoms. Yep, the same electrons and atoms that help a pelican find its way home and make your heart beat and give shape and substance to everything in the universe. Including you.

And that's the SHOCKING TRUTH!

SEE YA!

SHOCKING ELECTRICITY

QUIZ

**Now find out if you're a
Shocking Electricity expert!**

Electrical impulses are everywhere. In the Earth, in the clouds – even in your horrible science teacher. Without electricity there'd be no light bulbs, no television, nothing fun at all. Take these quick quizzes to see how much you really know about this fatal force…

ASTONISHING ELECTRONS

If your brain is fully switched on by this book, you'll know by now that electricity is made of electrons – tiny blips that spend their lives whizzing around the nucleus of atoms. But what do you really know about these powerful particles and their amazing effects?

1 What charge does an electron have?
a) Positive
b) Negative
c) Dangerous

WHY DO I FEEL SO NEGATIVE?

2 What is the name of the particle given out by electrons as they lose energy and slow down?
a) Pooton
b) Proton
c) Photon

3 What is static electricity?
a) A form of electricity in which the electrons stop moving completely.
b) A form of electricity in which electrons are transferred from one thing to another. changing the electrical charge of each.

c) A form of electricity that looks all fuzzy through a microscope.

4 How can you rearrange the atoms in a magnet so that it doesn't work any more?
a) By frying it over a strong heat.
b) By drowning it in salty water.
c) By slicing it in half with a chainsaw.

5 How do batteries make an electric current?
a) By removing all the positive charges from the metal casing.
b) By mixing two chemicals together.
c) By squashing together lots of tiny magnets.

6 What happens when you hold an electrified object?
a) Your muscles squeeze together so you can't let go and you'll probably die a horrible death.
b) It interrupts the electrical impulses in the heart and you'll probably die a horrible death.
c) The electricity fries your brain and you'll definitely die a horrible death.

7 Where is the safest place to shelter during an electric storm?
a) In a car.
b) Under a tree.
c) Under an umbrella.

8 How fast can electrons move?
a) About the speed of sound.
b) About the speed of a horse.
c) About the speed of light.

Answers:
1b; 2c; 3b; 4a; 5b; 6a; 7a; 8c

HORRIBLE ELECTRICITY FACTS

Electricity flows all around us (as well as inside us), but it took scientists a long time to get to grips with it, and along the way they made some messy mistakes. Below are some silly statements about electricity – can you figure out if these fascinating force facts are true or false?

1 Electricity flows from positively charged areas to negatively charged areas.
2 You can make electricity from farts.
3 Animals like sharks and bees can detect electrical pulses in humans.
4 Electricity always finds the quickest route to the ground.
5 Electricity can travel through metal wires.
6 Electric shocks aren't always bad – they can be used to re-start the heart if it stops beating.
7 The Earth is just one great big magnet.
8 The human body contains enough electricity to light the fairy lights on a Christmas tree.

Answers:

1 False. It's the other way around (although brilliant Ben Franklin got this wrong too…).

2 True. Farts contain the gas methane, which can power generators.

3 True. And it can make them pretty angry!

4 True. Which is why it's not a good idea to stand under an umbrella in a lightning storm – the metal in the umbrella will attract the electricity and channel is straight to the ground – through you!

5 False. Ha ha. Trick question – in fact, electricity travels through a field around the wire.

6 True. Doctors use a shockingly clever machine called a defibrillator that passes an electric current into the heart to restart it.

7 True. The Earth's core is surrounded by a massive sea of melted metal that sends out electric and magnetic forces.

8 True. But don't worry – if you weren't a bundle of electric pulses you'd be, well, dead.

STRANGE SCIENTISTS

They say it takes all sorts, but the silly scientists who helped us understand electricity were some of the strangest ever. Experiments with electricity can be horribly dangerous, and some of these fantastic physicists diced with death. Just take this quiz and find out for yourself...

1 What natural force did barmy Benjamin Franklin investigate in his most famous experiment? (Clue: It was certainly enlightening.)

2 What did John Joseph Thomson use to bend the ray of electrons in his cathode ray tube experiment? (Clue: It was an attractive experiment.)

3 What kind of electricity did ancient Greek Thales of Miletus experiment with? (Clue: It was certainly hair-raising.)

4 What amazing invention did Robert Van de Graf come up with? (Clue: It generated some interest at the time.)

5 What happened when Luigi Galvani attached his dead pet frog to the iron bars on his windows? (Clue: It made the silly scientist jump!)

6 What substance did Alessandro Volta find to be the best conductor for passing an electric current between two pieces of metal? (Clue: Water surprise!)

7 What magnetic mystery did William Gilbert solve while playing around with his compass? (Clue: He remained well-grounded despite his discovery.)

8 What magnificent machine did mad Michael Faraday build? (Clue: He was driven to it.)

Answers:
1 Lightning.
2 A magnet.
3 Static electricity.
4 An electrical generator.
5 The frog's legs jumped around as if it was still alive.
6 Salt water.
7 That the Earth is magnetic.
8 The electric motor.

MYSTERIOUS MEASUREMENTS

There are all sorts of ways of measuring electricity and most of the units of measurement are named after the strange scientists who discovered them. You've met some of them in this book, so now see if you can match the mad measurement with its meaning.

1 Amp
2 Volt
3 Watt
4 Ohm
5 Farad
6 Watthour
7 Coulomb
8 Henry

a) A measure of electrical resistance.
b) A measure of electrical storage capacity.
c) A measure of electric current.
d) A measure of electrical energy.
e) A measure of reaction to changes in the magnetic field.
f) A measure of electrical pressure.
g) A measure of electrical charge.
h) A measure of electrical power.

Answers:
1c; 2f; 3h; 4a; 5b; 6d; 7g; 8e

HORRIBLE INDEX

HORRIBLE SCIENCE

NASTY NATURE

I LOVE FAST FOOD!

NICK ARNOLD *illustrated by* TONY DE SAULLES

ISBN 978 0439 94451 9

HORRIBLE SCIENCE

DISGUSTING DIGESTION

IT TAKES GUTS!

NICK ARNOLD *illustrated by* TONY DE SAULLES

ISBN 978 0439 94445 8

HORRIBLE SCIENCE

UGLY BUGS

NOT A PRETTY SIGHT!

NICK ARNOLD *illustrated by* TONY DE SAULLES

ISBN 978 0439 94452 6